The Spanish Civil War

The Spanish Civil War

Edited with an Introduction by

Gabriel Jackson

A NEW YORK TIMES BOOK

Quadrangle Books
CHICAGO

Library of Congress Catalog Card Number: 78-182510
International Standard Book Number:
  Cloth 0-8129-0247-5
  Paper 0-8129-6190-0

The publishers are grateful to the contributors herein
for permission to reprint their articles.

Contents

Introduction   *3*

1. Background to Conflict

Party Struggles in Spain   *23*
  by *Frank E. Manuel*
Spain Faces Prospect of Long Class Battle   *30*
  by *Edwin L. James*
Spain at Her Great Decision   *35*
  by *Anita Brenner*

2. The War

Death in the Afternoon—and at Dawn   *45*
  by *Frank L. Kluckhohn*
Under the Death-spurting Skies of War-torn Madrid   *52*
  by *Herbert L. Matthews*

THE BATTLE OF BRUNETE

Great Battle in View as Government Adds to Gains   *61*
   by Herbert L. Matthews
Franco Says Drive of Foe Is a Failure   *64*
   by William P. Carney
Loyalist Advance Continues   *66*
   by Herbert L. Matthews
Rebels in Brunete After Hard Battle   *67*
   by Herbert L. Matthews
Taking of Teruel Upsets Prophecies   *71*
   by Hanson W. Baldwin
Behind the Battle Lines in a Devastated Spain   *75*
   by Alfred Winslow Jones
The Nationalists Enter Barcelona   *81*

3. Internal Politics

Sketches of the International Brigades   *92*
   by Herbert L. Matthews

Uncensored Report on the Siege of Madrid   *101*
   by William P. Carney

Anti-Stalin Chief Is Slain in Madrid   *125*

Revolt Threatens Spain's Loyalists   *129*
   by Herbert L. Matthews

Anarchism: Spain's Enigma   *133*
   by Herbert L. Matthews

Catalans Wooing Industrial Exiles   *140*
   by Lawrence A. Fernsworth

Fascist Influence in Spain Growing   *144*
   by Harold Callender

The Casado Coup in Madrid   *149*

4. Foreign Repercussions

Foreign Stakes Big in Spain   *155*
  by Lansing Warren
THE BOMBING OF THE DEUTSCHLAND
—BY SIX REPORTERS
Soviet Plot Is Seen in Berlin   *158*
  by Eugene J. Young
Fascist and Communist Powers Draw Back from
a War over Spain   *162*
  by Arnaldo Cortesi, Guido Enderis, and Harold Denny
Spanish Foes Unshaken by Setbacks   *168*
  by William P. Carney and Herbert L. Matthews

DEALING WITH MEDITERRANEAN PIRACY   *173*
At Nyon   *173*
Agreement Reached at Nyon   *177*
  by P. J. Philip

5. The Development of Nationalist Spain

Franco Financed Without a Loan   *186*
  by Harold Callender

Vignettes of Franco Spain   *190*
  by Harold Callender

Franco's Spain Twenty Years Later   *196*
  by Hugh Trevor-Roper

Suggested Reading   *205*

Index   *207*

The Spanish Civil War

Introduction

THE SPANISH CIVIL WAR of 1936–1939 was the climactic encounter in the struggle between revolutionary and traditionalist forces which had been taking place in Spain for well over a century. The partial reforms of Charles III in the late eighteenth century, and the resistance to the Napoleonic occupation in 1808, had both shown that there was a "red" Spain (favoring religious and political liberty, and an end to aristocratic privilege) face to face with a "black" Spain (favoring authoritarian, Catholic monarchy and the maintenance of the social hierarchies of the era before the French Revolution). The Carlist wars, the military uprisings (the *pronunciamientos* for which Spain was famous in the mid-nineteenth century), and the quasi-constitutional methods of the monarchy between 1876 and 1923, all attempted to provide some solution for the struggle between the "red" and the "black" Spains. After the loss of the Spanish-American War in 1898, and especially after the disastrous defeat of a Spanish expeditionary force in Morocco in 1921, the army increasingly intervened against the liberal and revolutionary forces, and Spain was ruled between 1923 and 1930 by a nonideological, humanly decent, military dictator, General Miguel Primo de Rivera. In 1931, with the installation of a parliamentary republic, it seemed as though "red" Spain had triumphed. But the military revolt of General Sanjurjo in 1932, and the revolt of the Catalan regionalists and the Asturian miners in 1934, indicated that neither reactionaries nor liberals nor leftist revolutionaries were ready to abide by constitutional, peaceful means for the settlement of their long-standing conflicts.

The active social forces which made up the Spanish Left in 1936 ran the gamut from "New Deal"–type republicans to revolutionary socialists, communists, and anarchists. The largest and probably most powerful single force was the socialist-led and communist-influenced General Union of Workers (UGT), which included more than a million industrial workers and miners, mostly in Castile, Andalusia, and northern Spain. The UGT had also recently begun to organize the landless peasants. Next in importance was the anarchist-led National Confederation of Labor (CNT), which counted approximately one million followers, mostly in Aragon, Catalonia, and the Mediterranean coastal cities. A prominent movement of middle-class republicans was more important in ability and prestige than in numbers, and was internally divided between Catholic and secular republicans. There was also a strong regional autonomist movement in Catalonia, whose principal leaders allied it with the liberal republicans and the two labor federations.

The Spanish Right was weaker than the Left in terms of popular mass organization, but it was considerably stronger in terms of economic power, administrative and political talent, and internal discipline. Its largest unit was the Confederation of Autonomous Right parties (CEDA), composed of conservative middle-class and peasant parties whose common bond was the defense of the historic privileges of the Catholic Church. Next in importance were the monarchists, divided between the adherents of the exiled King Alfonso XIII and those of the Carlist Pretender. The monarchists counted among their supporters most of the titled families, the large landowners, the principal bank and corporation directors, and a solid majority of the judges, high civil servants, and diplomats. The most prestigious army officers and bishops also supported the Right, whether or not they were concerned with monarchy as a form of government. Finally, the Right included a small but aggressive and rapidly growing fascist party, the *Falange.*

During the electoral campaign of February 1936, the Left formed a coalition of the liberal republican, Socialist, and Communist parties, the so-called Popular Front. In order to reassure alarmed conservatives, both Marxist parties stipulated that in the event of victory they would not enter the government but would support its program in the Cortes, the representative assembly. The agreed-upon program included full political and religious liberty, regional autonomy, reduction of the military forces, rapid land reform, the extension of school building, and various social services. But undoubtedly its single most important item was the promise of amnesty for the political prisoners who had been jailed after the Catalan and Asturian revolts of October 1934.

Under the leadership of the Left Republican Manuel Azaña, the Popular Front won some 257 out of a possible 473 Cortes seats (twenty more than an absolute majority) on February 16, 1936. The Right coalition, led by the prominent Catholic lawyer José María Gil Robles, had campaigned essentially on a "law and order" platform. While Gil Robles and other Right leaders conceded the loss of a valid election, many high military officers, among them General Francisco Franco, chief of the general staff, were openly critical when the government refused to declare martial law in order to prevent a Popular Front cabinet from taking office. From February until the outbreak of the Civil War in July, everyone knew that the militant Right was plotting to overthrow the Popular Front government. High military officers justified their plotting with the argument that in time of crisis the army was the final depository of national sovereignty, while monarchists were convinced that only Spain's traditional form of government, monarchy, could maintain civil peace.

The principal anti-government rallying cry was the restoration of public order, and much of the behavior of the revolutionary socialists and the anarchists played into the hands of the Right. Repeated strike waves raised the general level of public anxiety, and not a few publications indicated that both UGT and CNT looked upon the "bourgeois" Popular Front government only as a transitional regime on the road to some form of proletarian and collectivist rule. The irreconcilable differences between Marxists and anarchists, and the fact that much of the Socialist party remained fully committed to parliamentary methods, meant that in fact the Left was too disunited to launch a revolution in the foreseeable future. Moreover, the moderate wing of the Popular Front was greatly bolstered by the attitude of the Basque Nationalists. Their autonomy movement had developed more slowly than that of the Catalans. Their leaders were middle-class Catholics whose general ethos owed much to their business and family connections in France and England. The Basques had not joined the Popular Front, but they had refused the leadership of Gil Robles and were utterly opposed to military rule. Neither in the Basque country (nor in Catalonia) was there any threat of proletarian revolution during the spring of 1936. But in Madrid and in the southern provinces some of the revolutionary oratory, taken together with truculent parades, illegal land seizures, and a wave of church burnings, provided substantial justification for the attack on the government as being incapable of maintaining public order.

A well-planned military rising had already been scheduled for the period July 10-20 when the assassinations, on July 12, of a leftist Lieutenant José Castillo and of the monarchist leader José Calvo Sotelo, precipitated the outbreak of civil war. On July 18-19 the military rose in all portions of Spanish territory. They were immediately successful in the Canary Islands, Morocco, and Majorca, in the mainland provinces of Galicia and Navarre, and in large parts of Castile, Aragon, and Andalusia. But in Barcelona and Madrid, the two principal cities, hastily armed workers, led by loyal military and police officers, defeated the *pronunciamiento*. In Bilbao, where the civilian officials had routed all military telephone calls through the municipal switchboard, no rising occurred, and the Basque autonomous government, composed of ardent Catholics, took the side of the Popular Front against the military revolt.

The Insurgent generals could not have failed to realize that public sentiment did not favor a military dictatorship. Even their local victories, outside of Navarre and rural Castile, had been won by surprise and terror, involving the arrest of fellow officers and of civilian officials, the machine-gunning of working-class districts, the summary execution of UGT and CNT leaders, and the trick use of the slogan "Viva la República." Moreover, their best-armed units were located in Morocco, across the straits of Gibraltar, and were cut off from the mainland by naval units whose seamen had murdered their officers when the latter had tried to join the rising.

The generals had planned for a quick and not too bloody coup, but they now faced the prospect of at least a short war, for which their arms and transport were totally inadequate. During the planning stages they had made unofficial friendly contacts in Portugal, Italy, Germany, and England. (Franco had flown from the Canaries to Morocco in a private English plane, and the Insurgents were hoping for informal naval aid from Gibraltar.) On July 19 Franco sent an emissary to Mussolini to request twelve bombers and three fighter planes, and on July 22 he sent a request for ten transport planes to Germany. The general's brother, Nicolás Franco, and the millionaire tobacco smuggler Juan March established headquarters in Lisbon where the Salazar government treated them, rather than the Republican ambassador, as the official representatives of Spain. By July 30 the first German and Italian planes had reached Morocco, and by August 5 General Franco was ready to transport the army of Africa to southern Andalusia, where General Queipo de Llano had seized the city of Seville.

Meanwhile, on July 20 the Left Republican government of José Giral appealed to France for aid and in the first days of August received some twenty Potez aircraft. The Spanish Civil War was thus very rapidly internationalized. The Republicans, or Loyalists, as they were referred to in the international press, claimed the sympathy primarily of France, which had a Popular Front government under a Socialist premier, Léon Blum; and it hoped that all democratic countries would identify themselves with it as both a fellow democracy and a legitimately constituted government defending itself against military rebellion and fascist intervention. The Giral government hoped also for Soviet aid. Before Hitler had come to power in 1933, the German Communists had behaved as though the Socialists were worse enemies than the Nazis. Now the desire to unify the Left within each country coincided with Stalin's desire to form a diplomatic and perhaps military alliance with the Western democracies in order to "contain" Hitler. As a result the world congress of the Communist International in 1935 launched the movement for a popular front of all democratic and Marxist parties to prevent the further spread of fascism. Both the Spanish and French Popular Front governments were the result in part of that initiative by the Communist International.

Once the army of Africa had been ferried across the straits the Insurgents made rapid progress. These fifteen to twenty thousand moors and foreign legionnaires were among the world's toughest, best-disciplined troops. Advancing in columns of five hundred to a thousand, truck-borne, with plentiful supplies of machine guns and light artillery, their very appearance sowed terror in the countryside. Behind village walls, or gravestones, or within occasional stone buildings (often churches), a hastily gathered and poorly armed militia would resist desperately, and would frequently take a heavy toll of their overconfident attackers. When entirely surrounded they might fight to the last man. When escape seemed possible they would flee in bunches, along the open road, having no idea of the value of dispersal or of the firepower of machine guns. By August 14 the Insurgents had reached Badajoz, and by September 3 they were in Talavera. Here, by personal decision of General Franco, they turned aside from the direct route to Madrid in order to capture Toledo. In the city of El Greco the rising had been defeated by left-wing militia, but about one thousand Insurgents had retreated into the local fortress, the Alcazar, taking with them as hostages the families of some of the leftist militiamen. Since late July they had been under siege, and both the Spanish and the international press had attached great symbolic importance to the Alcazar. For Insurgent sympathizers it symbolized the heroic refusal of self-sacrificing "cadets" to surrender in the face of overwhelming odds and the likely prospect of starvation. For the Republicans it symbolized their own military incompetence and the fascist use of hostages. It was a great military and moral triumph for the Insurgents when Franco's army rescued the beleaguered garrison on September 28.

Meanwhile, arms from Germany and Italy had been unloaded in Portuguese ports and had been transported to the Spanish frontier with the full cooperation of the Portuguese government. At first these supplies had gone principally to the swift-moving army of Africa, but by mid-September trucks, gasoline, and armament of all kinds were also reaching the troops of General Mola, who had dug in on the crests of the Somosierra north of Madrid. After the relief of the Alcazar it looked as though the Insurgent armies would march into Madrid almost at will, not only because they were so much better trained and armed, but because the capital was inundated by half-starved refugees spreading stories of moorish atrocities and governmental incompetence. But the rate of advance now slowed considerably. The combat troops were tired. Their supply lines were long and their flanks dangerously exposed. Given their small numbers, casualties had been heavy, and many troops were needed to control a hostile countryside once the main attacking force had moved ahead. Madrid was not a village or a provincial capital. It was a city of one million, with labyrinthine streets, cement buildings, and stone pavements available for barricade construction. Within it the UGT and the Communist party had transformed metal shops into grenade factories, given thousands of ardent workers the rudiments of military training, and provided some combat experience against Mola's detachments in the Sierra. Soviet freighters by early October were unloading planes, tanks, and small arms in the Republican-held Mediterranean ports. On October 24 Russian tanks participated in a flank attack against the Insurgents south of Madrid, and on November 2 their fighter planes appeared over the city.

The Insurgents nevertheless expected to take Madrid in the first week of November—and the government, thinking likewise, hastily departed for Valencia on November 6. While General Mola talked of celebrating the anniversary of the Bolshevik Revolution (November 7) in Madrid, and while the War Ministry received telegrams congratulating General Franco on entering the capital, the Socialist, Communist, and anarchist militia, commanded by a few

dozen middle-rank professional officers, beat back the initial onslaught against the western approaches to the city. Simultaneously,
under the leadership of General José Miaja and Major Vicente
Rojo, the population built barricades, manned communications
posts, established soup kitchens, and rushed reinforcements (un-
armed men and a sprinkling of girls) to the most threatened
sectors of the front, where they would pick up rifles from the
wounded or the dead. On November 7 it looked as though the
attackers might penetrate the capital via the University City, but
on November 8 some two to three thousand volunteers from all
over Europe, the first of the famous International Brigades,
stemmed the advance in the University City. For another ten days
the Insurgents strained every fiber to maintain their momentum,
but by November 18 it was clear that they would not be able
soon, and by such tactics, to capture the city.

Although all the European nations had strong feelings about
events in Spain, they were anxious that the Civil War not "escalate"
into a general war. The Blum government in France had at first
responded to the Republicans by sending a few dozen obsolete
but serviceable planes. But the French Right was outraged by
this action, and when Blum consulted the British it was clear that
the Baldwin government's sympathies tended more toward the Insurgent side and that Britain would not defend France against
such retaliatory action as the Germans might take. Germany had
marched unopposed into the Rhineland four months earlier. No
matter what were the sentiments of the Popular Front majority, no
matter what were the strategic considerations at the Pyrenean
border or in north Africa, French security depended absolutely
on British cooperation. With British backing France now invited
all European nations to join in a common policy of "nonintervention," and on August 8 she closed her own frontier to military
traffic. Having to align herself with England, but hoping for a
Republican victory, she reasoned that if neither side could import
arms the Insurgent cause would die for lack of popular support.
Germany, Italy, and Portugal were aware of the same possibility.
They therefore armed the Insurgents as rapidly as they could
while stalling on the diplomatic front. They agreed to noninter-

vention "in principle" on August 24. The first meeting of the Non-Intervention Committee occurred in London on September 9, and on procedural grounds the committee refused on September 28 to hear charges against Portugal. On October 6 the Soviets announced they would not be more bound by the agreement than were the other parties thereto, and by late October their supplies, along with tank crews, pilots, and staff officers, were arriving in time to defend Madrid. Thus Italy, Germany, and Portugal were disappointed in their hope for a quick victory based on the aid which they had given since late July.

A further dimension had been added to the civil war in these first months by the occurrence of revolution in the Republican zone and of counterrevolution in the Insurgent zone. The factories of Catalonia, and all hotels, restaurants, and public services throughout the Republican zone (with the exception of the Basque country) were collectivized. Their new executive committees included members of all parties to the Popular Front and of both labor federations, and they retained the services of most of the management personnel who had not fled or been shot. Large agricultural areas of Aragon and New Castile were also collectivized. The more prosperous peasants of coastal Catalonia and Valencia resisted the surrender of their land but cooperated with collectivized transport, harvesting, and marketing arrangements (many of which were familiar practices in new ideological guise). Tipping was abolished everywhere, currency was eliminated in many villages, and for the first months of the war in revolutionary Catalonia, hats and other forms of "bourgeois" dress disappeared. The strongest single impulse of this revolution was not so much any particular form of social organization as it was decentralized, local, and popular control of all activities. It was accompanied also by terror. "Bosses" (rather than absentee or little-known factory and landowners), priests, Civil Guards, Falangists, and strike-breakers were the principal categories of victim. In the main cities the jails were raided and a number of prominent political prisoners lynched. Altogether, various forms of "red" terror claimed perhaps twenty thousand victims during the war, most of them between July and November 1936. The Republican government did what it could to reduce the terror, counseling people by radio not to open their doors at night to strangers, supplying professional judges for popular tribunals, permitting the wide extension of asylum in foreign embassies and consulates, and freely issuing passports to threatened families.

The establishment of authority in the Insurgent zone was regularly accompanied by counterrevolution and terror. The land reform of the preceding four years was canceled, strikes were forbidden, all political parties except the Carlists and the Falange were proscribed, and the press was tightly controlled. The army of Africa, being small in numbers and moving rapidly, had no time to take prisoners. Resisting militiamen were legally considered to be criminals caught with arms in hand, and were shot. The same treatment was given to those whose blue shoulder bruises indicated that they might recently have held a rifle. Resources and businesses were requisitioned without being confiscated. For the most part their managers, both Spanish and foreign, cooperated willingly with the military authorities. UGT and CNT militants were imprisoned, and many of their leaders shot. The "white" terror involved very little disorder since it was administered mostly by the military authorities. Absolutely no political asylum or voluntary emigration was countenanced. Executions continued throughout the war. They may have totaled close to 200,000; they were in any case fully as numerous as were deaths in battle. The above-described revolution and counterrevolution took place among a population far more politicized than that of 1917 Russia, and probably more politicized than that of the American colonies in 1776 or of France in 1789. This feeling of articulated aims, of limitless commitment, and of pitiless struggle, goes far to explain world fascination with the Spanish Civil War and the fact that it lasted for thirty-two months.

The successful defense of Madrid altered the entire military outlook. It was now clear that the Insurgents could not win quickly, nor without greatly increased aid from the Axis powers. On November 18 the Axis extended diplomatic recognition to Franco's government and made clear in both words and action that they would do whatever was necessary to guarantee his victory. During 1937 Italy sent anywhere from sixty to a hundred thousand soldiers, mostly infantrymen, supplied hundreds of planes, bombed Barcelona without Franco's permission, and used her navy on behalf of the Insurgents. Germany sent about twenty thousand men in relays, with perhaps half that number available at any one time as tank crews, pilots, and artillery and communications specialists using German-supplied armament. Portugal offered perhaps twenty thousand soldiers, but more importantly gave eager cooperation on port facilities, overland transport, diplomatic, and political police aid.

On February 10 the Insurgents took Malaga with an army which included some five thousand Italians. Simultaneously they attempted to encircle Madrid from the south, but the Jarama River offensive ended in bloody stalemate. On March 8 they opened a drive from north of the capital with fifty thousand troops, of whom about thirty thousand were Italians, and with Italian generals in command. A combination of bad weather, poor staff work, and Republican prowess defeated this offensive, known as the Battle of Guadalajara. The Insurgents, not unhappy at Italian discomfiture, then turned to the northern front where the Basques were well dug in and highly disciplined, but where both food and arms were running short. On April 26 German planes, experimenting with different types of explosive and incendiary bombs, and interested as much in terrorizing the civilian populace as in striking military objectives, destroyed the medieval Basque capital, the town of Guernica. A cry of moral outrage resounded throughout the democratic world. The Insurgents and the Axis were perhaps surprised, since Italy had done similar things in Ethiopia in 1935 and since the Condor Legion had bombed another Basque town, Durango, almost as heavily. The Insurgents brazenly announced that the "reds" had burnt the city, and Guernica came rapidly to symbolize two of the most outstanding qualities of the fascist-dictatorial mentality: massive terror and "the big lie."

Advancing slowly but inexorably, the Insurgents captured Bilbao on June 19. In an effort to relieve the pressure on the remaining northern provinces and to prove the offensive capability of their army, the Republicans launched an attack northwest of Madrid. But the Battle of Brunete, July 7-26, entailed heavy casualties without greatly delaying the conquest of the north. On August 26 the Insurgents took Santander, and on October 19 their capture of Gijon ended all but minor guerrilla resistance in northern Spain. Generally speaking, in the 1937 campaigns the Insurgents gained considerable territory but could not force a decision. The Republican army did not have either the equipment or the professional officers to sustain an offensive, but it had become a disciplined force capable of tactical successes, and able to hold its own on the defensive.

During the same year General Franco, for all his caution, his lack of military genius, and his previous unfamiliarity with economic questions, established himself as the very able master of what the world press increasingly referred to as Nationalist Spain. On April 19 he nipped political revolt in the bud by unifying the Falange and the Carlists—the two permitted political forces in his territory—under his personal leadership. He astutely postponed the decision to return postwar Spain to a monarchy. He made the best use of his ardent following among midde-class youth by training them as combat officers. He completed favorable trading arrangements with British and American firms (Texaco, Ford, and Studebaker all sold oil and trucks to Franco, these items not being embargoed under U.S. neutrality laws). He made minimal economic concessions to Germany. He was able adequately to feed his zone, to get Basque industry producing fully within a few months of the capture of Bilbao, to bring 1937 exports from Nationalist Spain almost to the level of total Spanish exports in 1935, and to hold the Nationalist peseta much closer to its theoretical exchange value than the Republican peseta. He enjoyed the strong support of the Church hierarchy without in any way placing himself under the tutelage of the bishops.

In all this he was greatly helped by international developments. All Spain's wealthy conservatives used their money and their connections to see to it that the international business community aided the Nationalist cause. British and French conservatives were somewhat divided in their sympathies as long as there was an independent, socially and economically conservative, Basque government. But after the fall of Bilbao they were eager for a Franco victory. Similar considerations applied to the Vatican, which had refused to condemn the Basques, and indeed had been disturbed by Nationalist treatment of the Basque clergy. But after the end of Basque resistance the Vatican became singlemindedly committed to Franco, and the collective letter of the Spanish hierarchy in July 1937 gave him the most solemn support of the Spanish Church. His international position also benefited greatly from the diplomatic attitude of the British. At all meetings of the Non-Intervention Committee the chairman, Lord Plymouth, used every procedural means to protect the Axis from any substantive discussion of their aid to Franco while engaging in repeated condemnations of the quantitatively much smaller Soviet aid to the Republic. Even when piracy by Italian submarines moved England to place limits on Mussolini's impudence, the British-sponsored Nyon agreements which ended Italian submarine attacks on British and Russian freighters did not in any way interfere with Italy's supply of men and arms to Franco.

During 1937 the Republic, on the other hand, was able to train, house, feed, and partially equip a highly motivated army of five to six hundred thousand men. Soviet Russia sent guns, tanks, and planes in something less than half the quantity delivered to the Insurgents. About thirty thousand volunteers in the International Brigades, of whom five to six thousand were available at any given time, played a major role at Guadalajara and acted as spearheads in the Brunete and brief Aragon offensives. Some two thousand Soviet personnel were a mixed blessing: pilots, tank drivers, and some staff officers were invaluable, but Russian tank tactics, Russian insistence on the Brunete offensive, and Russian interference in Republican politics were all negative factors.

At the same time the Republic was unable to achieve the unity and discipline that Franco had built in his portion of Spain. As Prime Minister from September 1936 to May 1937, Largo Caballero presided over the conversion of undisciplined political militia units into a disciplined Republican army. He had gotten anarchists to work in the government and army side by side with Socialists, Communists, and republicans. But under the surface, enmities were hardening, principally over the role of the Communist party and of the Soviet advisers. The party insisted that everything else must be subordinated to fighting the war. Social revolution must be curbed in the interest of efficiency and in order to win England and France to the concept of collective security, after which they would, hopefully, sell arms to the Republic. The parliamentary Socialists and most of the republicans agreed with the Communist position. The anarchists and the left Socialists felt that a continuing social revolution was necessary in order for the war itself to be worth fighting. The Catalan regional government was afraid its own autonomy would be destroyed in proportion as Communist power increased.

This ideological conflict was exacerbated by the political purges taking place in the Soviet Union. One of the small but vigorous parties in Catalonia was the POUM, an anti-Stalinist Marxist party whose leader, Andrés Nin, had once been Leon Trotsky's secretary and who remained an admirer though not an uncritical follower of the exiled Russian leader. Stalin was determined to eradicate "Trotskyite vermin" in Spain as well as in Russia, and the POUM (along with the anarchists) was determined that the Soviets should not destroy the collectivist revolution in Catalonia and rural Aragon. The internal conflict came to a head in several days of street fighting in Barcelona in early May 1937. Communists and Socialists faced the anarchists and the POUM. Largo Caballero and the Catalan regional government hoped to end the fighting without splitting the Left. But the anarchist ministers whom Largo sent to negotiate in Barcelona could not get a hearing from their own followers. At the same time the Communists were determined to crush the revolutionaries and were not unhappy to discredit the Prime Minister in the process.

On May 17 the moderate Socialist Juan Negrín replaced Largo Caballero as Prime Minister. Negrín was a physiologist of international reputation, and an immensely able executive. He admired Communist efficiency and faced realistically his dependence on Soviet supplies. He reasoned that sooner or later the Western democracies would, in the interest of their own survival, enter into collective-security arrangements with the Soviets. Meanwhile he must retain Soviet good will, keep an army in the field, and govern internally as a "bourgeois moderate." This meant arresting the POUM leaders, dissolving some of the anarchist collectives, and swallowing his rage when Soviet agents kidnaped and later murdered Andrés Nin. At the same time he refused Soviet pressure to merge the Socialist and Communist parties, restored Catholic services in the army, quickly released most of the POUM and anarchist prisoners, and in late 1938 exonerated the main leaders in a trial very different from those being conducted in Moscow.

In late 1937 all signs pointed toward a new Nationalist campaign against Madrid. In order to forestall it the Republic launched an offensive on December 15 at Teruel. They achieved surprise and tactical success under difficult conditions of weather and terrain. They also succeeded in their psychological calculation that General Franco would transfer troops and postpone his own offensive rather than allow the Republic to gain even a minor victory. As in all their offensives, however, they lacked the supplies and the trained reserves to maintain their advance once the enemy had brought up reinforcements. By February 22, 1938, the Nationalists had recaptured the city, and when Franco then launched a massive attack in Aragon on March 9, the Republican army could offer little resistance. On April 15 the Nationalists reached the Mediterranean, thereby splitting Republican Spain into two zones, but their own losses of men and equipment prevented them from delivering a knockout blow.

Now more than ever, international events determined the course of the struggle. On March 11 Hitler occupied Austria, and the French reopened the Pyrenean border, thus allowing the Republic to obtain new supplies which enabled them by mid-April to check the Nationalist advance. Through the spring and summer Hitler threatened Czechoslovakia. In late June the French again closed the frontier. On July 24 Negrín, having massed all available supplies for a new offensive, crossed the Ebro River, once again achieving surprise, raising Republican morale by the skill and courage of the operation, and forcing the Nationalists to spend three months regaining what the Republicans had taken in the first week of battle. While both sides showed superb fighting spirit, the Negrín and Franco governments anxiously awaited the outcome of the Czech crisis. If war came, Germany and Italy would have to abandon Franco in order to fight the Western powers and the Soviet Union, and Negrín would have won his gamble: to merge the cause of the Republic with the international defense against fascism. A worried General Franco assured France and England that he would be strictly neutral in case of war. But on October 1, at Munich, the Western powers delivered Czechoslovakia to Hitler and ended all hope of collective security by deliberately excluding the Soviet Union from the negotiations. The Munich pact broke the morale of the Spanish Republican army. At the same time it was followed by extensive new supplies for the Nationalists in return for mining concessions to Germany.

Meanwhile, in the course of 1938 General Franco had developed the political and institutional outlines of his new Spain. On January 30 he had named a largely civilian cabinet, in which monarchists, Falangists, and nonpolitical experts (some of whom had held high office during the Primo de Rivera dictatorship) were carefully balanced and the supreme personal authority of General Franco was explicitly recognized. In April this government officially revoked the Republican divorce law, the land reform, and the statute of Catalan autonomy. In October 1937 a papal nuncio had arrived in Burgos. From then on there was no question but what the Catholic Church would be fully reestablished as the official church of Spain, but the modalities of the new Concordat were not worked out until after the war. To all proposals for a mediated peace Franco issued blunt refusals, stating repeatedly that his enemies, whom he regarded as in rebellion against "National" Spain, would have to rely upon his justice. Except in the few weeks preceding the Munich pact he was always supremely confident of his eventual victory.

In January 1939 the rearmed Nationalists invaded Catalonia. The Republican army possessed virtually no artillery or planes. Direct Soviet shipments had ended in September 1937 when

Japanese incursions at the Siberian frontier had forced the Soviets
to concentrate on their own defenses, and the arms that had
crossed the French frontier between March and June 1938 had
been consumed in the Battle of the Ebro. The Nationalists occupied Tarragona on January 15 and entered Barcelona on the
26th. In the ensuing two weeks half a million Spaniards fled
across the French frontier, and on February 9 the Nationalists
completed the occupation of Catalonia. In the southern French
city of Toulouse, Negrín urged continued resistance, but President
Azaña resigned his office in frank acknowledgment of defeat, and
all the non-Communist military leaders, notably the ablest pro-
fessionals, Generals Rojo and Matallana, stated that further resistance was hopeless. But Negrín was not thinking solely of
military capabilities. The Nationalist Law of Political Responsibilities, announced on February 13, made liable to severe penalties
all Spaniards who had opposed the *movimiento nacional* since
October 1, 1934. Under such a broad definition everyone who had
ever favored the Popular Front might be treated as a criminal.
Feeling responsible for the fate of millions of soldiers and
civilians, the Prime Minister flew back to the central zone, hoping
with the support of the Communists to maintain resistance until,
at the very least, he could obtain surrender terms that would
guarantee the partisans of the Republic against political reprisals.
In Madrid Colonel Casado, supported by the moderate Socialist
Julián Besteiro, and eventually by General Miaja, thought he
could obtain better terms than Negrín. On March 5 he formed a
Council of National Defense. The Communists, without any encouragement from Negrín, for whom a civil war within the Republican zone was the final nightmare, resisted for several days.
Casado and Besteiro then tried to negotiate with Franco, but the
latter insisted, as he always had, on unconditional surrender. On
March 28 the Nationalists were welcomed into Madrid by a
semi-starved, war-weary population hoping desperately for a peace
of reconciliation. On April 1 the transfer of power was complete
throughout the country, and General Franco began to administer
the peace of victory to which he and his spokesmen had repeatedly
referred.

New York Times coverage of the Spanish Civil War reflected the intense world preoccupation with the struggle. It was remarkably accurate concerning the internal political development of both zones, and in following the diplomacy of "nonintervention." After the first few weeks neither side permitted correspondents in the battle zones, so that the coverage of ground action at Madrid, the Jarama, Brunete, Teruel, and the Ebro had to be based on official communiqués, which were nevertheless interpreted with considerable acumen. Some of the finest reporting had to do with the air raids and with living conditions behind the lines. Maximum attention was given between the outbreak of the war and the spring of 1937, the period of swiftest military action and also of revolution and counterrevolution. After the Insurgent failure to capture Madrid, a military stalemate developed. In September 1937 the Sino-Japanese War began to compete for the headlines, and from February to November 1938 the Nazi occupation of Austria followed by the Czechoslovak crisis and the Munich Pact overshadowed Spanish events. Furthermore, once Franco's armies had reached the Mediterranean in April 1938, the entire world, with the slight exception of the Spanish Republican army, considered the Nationalist victory inevitable.

Part 1

BACKGROUND TO CONFLICT

THE FOLLOWING three articles, published in the first days of the Civil War, offer an excellent general understanding of the issues. Frank Manuel's essay is particularly strong on the mutual attitudes of the government and the army, the role of Calvo Sotelo, the widespread anticipation of a fascist coup, and the political nuances especially on the Left. In stating that "this is the fourth time since 1931 that the workers have been called upon to save the republic," Manuel perhaps exaggerates the extent to which the workers actually supported the republic. E. L. James writes from a more conservative viewpoint, and is accurate in his emphasis on class warfare and on the inability of the government to handle the hostile military. He underlines the French stake, and seems not to be aware of the Italian, German, and Portuguese roles in aiding the rebels from the start. Anita Brenner's article is especially valuable for communicating the sense of drama, tension, and extraordinary political involvement of the people. She is excellent on the pendulum swings and the main problems of the 1931–1935 period, and on the "dual power" situation resulting from the February elections. There are slight errors to be noted. The acreage that landlords sometimes used only for pasture was often good for nothing else; army officers more frequently came from modest than from aristocratic families; and Gil Robles was a clerical reactionary but not a fascist.

Party Struggles
in Spain

by Frank E. Manuel

THE MILITARY UPRISING in Spain is the final outburst of latent
Fascist, clerical, and aristocratic forces which for many months
have sought to undermine the Left Republican government at
Madrid. Ever since the Popular Front, comprised of Syndicalists,
Communists, Socialists, and Republican parties, won its victory in
the elections of Feb. 16, there have been rumors that the army
would use force to annul the decision of the people. Grandees
who were being deprived of their landed estates, capitalists who
feared revolutionary measures in favor of workers' organizations,
and the Jesuits who had experienced an economic renaissance under a former Premier, Lerroux, were all at hand with ample funds
to finance the movement.

The Popular Front Ministry needed a strong arm in order to
forestall this attempt to destroy the democratic régime, but the
Left Republicans who formed the Cabinet did not dare to dis-
charge those military men whom it knew to be avowed enemies of
the State. Instead, the Ministry instituted a procedure, jocularly
called "turismo" by the army officers, which meant the transfer

of dangerous military elements from strategic positions to apparently less significant posts.

Warnings Available

When in May there was a military rebellion in the garrison of Alcala de Henares, a foretaste of the present civil strife, Premier Quiroga suppressed it with adequate speed and then was too magnanimous to demand severe punishment for the traitors. Important army officers frankly admitted that the majority of their fellows remained faithful to the monarchy and were toying with the Fascist ideas of young Primo de Rivera. When the government tried to find a hundred officers, whose republican sympathies it could trust implicitly, in order to station them at points of vantage throughout the country, its most ardent efforts brought out only sixty-odd men.

Thus, during the whole period since February, the Cabinet was well aware of the fact that it was living under the continual threat of an armed attack, but it did almost nothing.

In a desperate attempt to protect itself the Cabinet tried to station the most hostile forces outside of the peninsula. The Spanish military establishment in North Africa was necessarily extensive because there were always rumblings among the Moorish nationalists. Some of the more blatant anti-republicans were sent there to command the Foreign Legion. And it was precisely this army corps which initiated the insurrection with the capture of Ceuta.

Rebel Leaders Spared

Furthermore, the Left republican government maintained within its ranks two generals who were its most renowned adversaries. A story is current about the manner in which Manuel Azaña, as Prime Minister, dealt with General Franco, the present leader of the rebellion, during a previous escapade of minor proportions. The soldier was solemnly warned that his position in history would suffer if he continued to intrigue for administrative power; he was begged to serve his country and to leave politics alone;

then he was transferred to the Canary Islands to reflect upon the wisdom of this advice. For a similar offense General Goded, who has since led the rebel movement in Catalonia, was sent to the Balearic Islands.

These generals were thus allowed to hibernate under sunny skies and to prepare the present uprising. It was imagined that if they were removed from the immediate scene of political conflict in Madrid they would feel themselves duly chastised and would ultimately be won over to the republic. Instead, the enforced leisure of these military chieftains provided them with ample time to intrigue and to win to their side the late General Sanjurjo, the Lion of the Riff.

Plan of the Revolt

According to the plan worked out, General Franco hoped to advance from the south with his Moroccan troops, while General Goded landed at Barcelona, invaded Catalonia, and then moved on Madrid. Once in the capital the rebels would establish a military dictatorship after the manner of the old Primo de Rivera, dissolve the workers' unions and annihilate the Marxist political parties.

If Calvo Sotelo, the Monarchist leader, had not been assassinated before the revolt he would have served as the rebels' expert economic adviser, perhaps the only man in the whole movement who had the vaguest notion about the administrative functions of government. In an interview a few weeks before his death he avowed that 90 per cent of the Monarchists had become Fascists; his ideal government for Spain he identified as a cross between the Portuguese and the Italian types.

Scandals in the family of Alfonso XIII made it impossible to consider immediately an actual restoration of the monarchy. To the army men, Catholic reactionaries, and Monarchists, fascism means the imitation of the existing European models and the suppression of communism. The Spanish Phalanx of young Primo de Rivera was the official Fascist body, but support for this doctrine extended over all the parties of the Right.

The Spanish army has always felt itself to be the legitimate ruler of the country. Since there was no prospect of foreign aggression it naturally turned its soul toward the internal problems of the régime. The officers still conceived of Spain as a State where power was transferred from one group to another after a skirmish between opposing colonels and generals in the manner of numerous coups.

Fascist Hopes Raised

Events of the last two months made the army men sanguine. Internal dissensions within the ranks of the Popular Front nourished the hope of the Fascist leaders that they might be able to put over an old-fashioned military uprising. Strikes were sweeping the country and the government's arbitration boards settled none of them, in marked contrast with the decisive moves of Premier Blum in France.

The Anarcho-Syndicalists' National Federation of Labor was at odds with the General Union of Labor, which is composed of Socialists and Communists, and the struggles of these two bodies sometimes led to bloodshed. The Socialist party was facing a schism: one group, under Indalecio Prieto, demanded actual participation in the Left Republican Ministry, while another, under Largo Caballero, opposed this policy as vain reformism and preached a doctrine of revolutionary class struggle.

Violence Spreads

In towns all over the country there were daily assassinations, Fascists and Marxist workers wreaking vengeance upon each other. Strict censorship kept accounts of these incidents out of the newspapers, but the lack of specific information only intensified the spirit of unrest. The foreign press was feeding on stories of Spanish atrocities and the burning of a few churches was exaggerated a hundredfold.

Legislative activity in the Cortes was slow because the Ministers were harassed by labor conflicts. Debates on the political economy of the Canary Islands lasted for days. Parliamentary commissions could not work when the Deputies of the Right refused to attend meetings. Gil Robles and Calvo Sotelo were interrupting the program of social reform which the Popular Front had promised the people with long interpellations on public order. These Deputies of the Right could then paint the anarchy of the country in dramatic terms.

Fascist propaganda began to penetrate the villages and the Fascist salute made its appearance in competition with the clenched fist of the Popular Front. Everyone soon expressed discontent with the existing government. Each day brought its batch of general strikes and new stories of political murders. In the face of these disorders ex-Republican intellectuals like Miguel de Unamuno could remark rather hopefully: "Who knows what fascism in Spain may bring?" The scene seemed all prepared for a typical army rebellion and an easy victory.

Working Class Aroused

But the Fascists had underestimated the strength of the workers and the Marxist parties. Since the republic was first formed, in 1931, Socialist and Communist propaganda had completely metamorphosed the temper of the working class and had even made inroads into the ranks of anarcho-syndicalism, the traditional apolitical attitude of the Spanish proletariat. The Communists, whose official party membership rose from 22,000 in February to 150,000 in July, were consolidating their forces, uniting Socialist and Communist youth movements, and developing an armed militia among the workers. The proletariat was to protect the Republican régime even when the Cabinet seemed lax in its own defense.

The workers' parties wanted to support the republic in order first to achieve peacefully the program of the Popular Front, leaving more revolutionary action for the future. But the Marxists were also preparing themselves for the contingency of a Fascist coup.

After union meetings in the Casa del Pueblo (House of the

People) in Madrid there were collections of money for the purchase of arms. Workers whose salaries are notoriously low contributed their pittance. For days before the actual outbreak young members of the Communist militia stayed awake nights waiting to be called at any moment. Thus, when confronted by a common enemy the parties of the Popular Front forgot their internal quarrels and prepared to unite for action. When the military movement finally did occur, workers and peasants were ready to oppose it.

The Rebel Stronghold

The army chiefs made a successful advance through the southeast, because that district is sparsely settled, but from the first their hold on Seville was stoutly resisted. Their main strength may be marked in the northern provinces which lie to the west of Catalonia—the Basque country, Old Castile, and Navarre. Here the land has for years been divided among small peasant proprietors who could derive no advantage from the new agrarian reform. This is also the stronghold of the old Carlist frondeurs, who still exert some influence over the peasantry.

Weakness in the central government, an anti-clerical policy, an increase in taxation, legends that communism will destroy all property and nationalize women were the factors which won these peasants to the side of the rebels. And they are no mean force.

On the other hand, the cause of the army chiefs has been deeply hurt because they have not won the Civil Guards, contrary to what might have been expected.

The sympathies of these 40,000 Civil Guards, a corps with a discipline superior to that of the army, were always reputed to be on the extreme Right. Hence recent scenes during which these guards armed and directed peasants and workers in a loyal defense of the republic are among the surprises of the present Fascist putsch.

What of the Future?

War is still raging in Spain and any reflections upon the future outlook are hazardous. Yet it seems certain that a momentary Fascist victory would be followed by a long-drawn-out period of civil strife. Should the Republican government become disorganized the proletariat may even attempt to seize power in its own right.

This is the fourth time since 1931 that the workers have been called upon to save the republic. After each victory they have found reason to express their discontent with the policy pursued by a bourgeois government they had raised to office. What concessions will they now demand if they successfully preserve President Azaña from the vengeance of Franco and Goded? There is reason to presume that this time the workers will not surrender the arms which the government had to distribute among them in order to survive.

The Kerensky analogy, in spite of certain basic differences, continually recurs to one's mind.

Spain Faces Prospect of Long Class Battle

by Edwin L. James

IN SPAIN'S CLASS revolution as many men are said to have been killed as the A. E. F. lost in battle in France. As nearly as can be told from the conflicting claims, the revolting forces now hold half of the country. Despite the government's announcements of victories, the Premier admits that the rebels are at points within fifty miles from the capital, which with all train service suspended and its water supply in danger, faces the peril of being starved out.

It is no ordinary political fight which is in progress. It is not a customary struggle of those who are out against those who are in. It is a class war, the roots of which go deep. On the one side, there is the Popular Front which won a majority of the seats in the Cortes in last February's election. The government is composed of Left leaders whose strength is based on the support of people who run all the way from moderates to Communists. On the other side are the Monarchists, the land-owners and the Clericals, as well as a vast number of people who believe in the Spain that was and hate the prospects of the Spain which the Left government planned to build. It must be admitted that on the rebel side are those who for generations have been the leaders of the country. As the struggle looms, it is between those who would be called popularly reactionaries and those who might be called Marxists. Spain gives today the sorry spectacle of the limit to which may go political efforts to align class against class.

The whole country is disrupted by the feeling that in politics, in industry and in agriculture the interests of one part of the population bear no relation to the interests of the other.

The Broader Aspects

Premier Giral did not exaggerate when he said Friday that it was the most important struggle in Spain in 100 years and that the outcome would be far-reaching indeed. The effort to drive Spain into a country governed by Socialist principles ran up against forces which had the strength of tradition. The breaking up of the landed estates which had existed for centuries, the burning of hundreds of churches because young Communists detested the Jesuits—such things were resented by a large and able part of the population. The position of the Left government had the great weakness that the officers of the army hated what was being done. The government knew as much, but because doubtless of the long tradition of the prestige of the army's officers had hesitated to follow the facts of the situation to their logical conclusion. This or that general, suspected of disloyalty to a government which stood for things Spanish generals did not like, was sent to Morocco or to the Canary Islands instead of being dismissed. And it was precisely in the colonies that the present revolution started, although its scope and virulence showed that it had been organized well in many parts of the country.

While the future of Spain is at stake, the fight has taken on larger aspects in the Old World. That is natural in a continent divided between dictators, as far to the Right as they can get, and democracies, tending steadily to the Left. The implications are eloquently shown by the request of the Madrid Left government for aid from the French Left government. Too much importance should not be attached to the delivery of fifteen bombing planes to Madrid; they were ordered months ago. But now a different tone is given the situation by Madrid's request for thousands of air bombs, many more planes and large supplies of ammunition. There is even a report that the French Communists would organize a division to go fight the Spanish rebels.

The reaction in Paris is what was to be expected. The moderates are up in arms against any such undertaking and the Blum government faces the choice of refusing to help its political coreligionists in Spain or of intensifying the class contest in France. Furthermore, M. Blum will earn no gratitude in Berlin or Rome—or even in London—by taking steps which may turn out to be a help in the establishment of a Communist régime in Madrid.

Republic Is in Danger

Whoever wins in the present revolt, it is likely that some sort of Spanish dictatorship will replace the Republic, which has been in existence since Alfonso fled five years ago. Certainly if the army leaders of the revolt capture Madrid and establish their régime they are not going to be "bothered" with a parliament for the time being. There will be a military junta which would run the country. If the revolt is defeated, one may expect forms of repression which could not be carried out by a parliamentary government. It will be a long time before the Cortes, in session assembled, will be able to vote a Cabinet out of office. In other words, regardless of who wins, Spain is in for a long period of political difficulty and hostility. In the troubled waters the Communists may be expected to fish for what they can catch.

It is difficult to make any prediction now as to the outcome of the fighting. The rebels are in control of Valencia, Cacares, Zamora, Salamanca, Valladolid, Seville, Cordova, Burgos and Vitoria. The government claims control of Madrid, Toledo, Cuenca, Guadalajara, Bilbao, San Sebastian, Almeria and Catalonia. There are daily, almost hourly, shifts in position, and as this is written there are reports of the rebellion of army units in the capital.

Role of the Navy

Due to the importance of military supplies, a great deal depends on the attitude of the navy, which apparently has remained loyal to the Left régime. It is the navy which has prevented the transfer of the Foreign Legion and other troops from Morocco to the metropolitan area. If the navy remains loyal it is apparent that the government has a great and important protection it would lack should naval officers place their ships under the command of the rebels.

However, it is plain that, inasmuch as the Spanish marine was caught without large supplies of oil fuel, the navy will be in need of refueling. It is reported that the French will undertake the refueling of the Spanish Navy. That is probably an exaggeration put that way. If the Spanish warships are free to move about, they are free to buy fuel where they can, and in all likelihood will be able to do so. General Franco, himself, could not complain about that.

The main danger to the régime seems to be that insurrectionist forces are on three sides of Madrid, at distances of fifty miles on the north and sixty miles on the south. General Mola indicates that his tactics will be to try to bring Madrid to terms by isolating the capital rather than making frontal attacks. If he can cut off food supplies from the city, it is evident that he will have a strong weapon. As he puts it: "After all, it is better to bring Madrid to surrender by hunger than by cannon."

Tactics of Defenders

Evidently the defenders of Madrid fear the strategy of surrounding the city. There are constant reports of the dispatch of defenders from the capital to arrange resistance in mountain passes. The government announces bloody victories over the rebellious forces and tells of driving them back with heavy losses but the very mention of the locations of engagements shows there are many rebel forces within less than 100 miles of the capital in several directions.

Although Madrid is not the largest city in Spain, it is the traditional seat of government, and while its capture would not necessarily end the civil war it would have an enormous effect should General Mola and General Franco succeed in taking control of it. Especially is this true because the Leftist forces are stronger in the capital than anywhere else in the country.

The latest reports from Spain say that the government admits that the rebels hold twenty-eight of the fifty provinces of the country while the government holds twenty-two. If that is an indication, then it is anybody's war up to the present.

Naturally, all of Europe is watching the French reply to the Macedonian call from the Popular Front of Madrid. The effect of the Spanish struggle will be felt throughout the Old World; it will become of immensely greater international importance if France, or any other country, tries to take sides. It is believed that such a turn is not likely; if it does come about the reactions are difficult to measure.

Most statesmen will think it best for the Spanish to fight it out on their own lines and to their own conclusions.

Spain at Her Great Decision

by Anita Brenner

WHEN A WHOLE people transforms itself into a fighting force, makes arsenals of its homes, hospitals of its theatres and schools, snipers' nests of its towers and windows and battlefields of its streets, it is writing history on a scale of such magnitude that events cannot be described or grasped in terms of what happens from day to day.

Thus the civil war that in Spain cleaves every city, every town, indeed almost every family, in a struggle for control of the nation's powers, has actually been going on since long before the recent explosion. And this chronic warfare, now blazing, now smoldering, from border to border of the land, does not consist of armed encounters only. It takes a great many forms: strikes, riots, demonstrations and counter-demonstrations, gang warfare, political feuds and manoeuvres, trade and market manipulations and all the other phenomena of acute social-economic crisis.

The war in which practically every Spaniard is now a militant has been described as a combination of the English Reformation and the French Revolution. It is the two, and it also telescopes a great deal of more modern history: a large proportion of Russia, 1917, and of the Socialist-Fascist struggles now going on in several parts of the world.

In the five years since that Spring day when Alfonso XIII was voted off his throne and the republic arrived in a whirl of confetti and paper hats, there have been three Congresses, two Presidents and five major uprisings: two from the Right, three from the Left. Each has been bigger and more desperately pitched than the one before. Each has drawn in more groups and more towns; so that now every place, every idea, every loyalty in the life of the people is, like the people themselves, a sharp, two-sided thing.

But two-sided only. Five years ago the political colors of Spain were broken into many shades. There were several kinds of Republicans, three or four kinds of Royalists, Fascists, Nationalists, Federalists, Separatists—as well as six or seven main branches of revolutionary doctrine professed by the organizations in which most peasants and workers were already enrolled.

Today the choice between throne and republic, as between different kinds of republics, is blurred and irrelevant. There are almost as few liberals who worry about political forms as Royalists willing to lay down their lives for a Bourbon.

Today each is violently a part of a single great contest. Today, if you are a Spaniard, you have almost forgotten what you called yourself in 1931. Today you pick up your gun and choose one of two sides, which you call Marxist and Fascist, revolutionary and counter-revolutionary. You do not care very much whether the government you support is called republic or dictatorship. What you risk your life to decide is not what kind of government you are going to have, but whose it shall be.

And, just as in the fighting itself the strategic points are telephone and telegraph buildings, radio and railroad stations, power plants, factories—rather than parliaments and palaces—so in the minds of the fighters the question of political power is identical with control of economic resources. The riots and strikes and annual rebellions since the birth of the republic all debouch at this point; and now the war has become decisive.

I

The story of the second Spanish Republic falls into chapters according as this question of economic control sharpens. The monarchy collapsed a year after the world crisis began, because it had not been able to meet the problem of how 23,000,000 Spaniards were all going to make a comfortable living. By 1930 there was no emergency margin left in the machinery of production. Spain had been in chronic crisis for many years and had already been provoked to the point of revolution by 1905, after the kingdom had lost its last American colony.

There were prophetic uprisings in 1909 and 1917. Another threatened in 1921, when Primo de Rivera took the government over and attempted to correct, dictatorially, the top-heavy burden that was so unendurable as to drive thousands of Spaniards away yearly, especially to the Americas.

When the post-war crisis shut almost every door to these emigrants, a revolution to readjust production and property—whether by decree from the top, as Primo de Rivera sought to bring it about, or by explosion from the bottom—became inevitable.

When the republic was proclaimed in April, 1931, the event was hailed everywhere as a bloodless revolution and was celebrated as madly as if the King, by his simple departure, had relieved the land of all its ancient ills. And there were many utopian republicans who believed it. Even Azaña, the most realistic republican in Spain, half hoped and half believed that the exercise of civil liberty, the opportunity to practice citizenship, in a free give-and-take manner, would adjust Spanish destinies; would assure every man the thing guaranteed him by the new Constitution—the right to work and to live "a dignified life."

Somehow the confetti and sunshine of April seemed to wipe from the minds of the "Men of the Republic" the fact that the new government had been heralded—indeed, determined—by a general strike and a military uprising just a few months before; also, that these events were in turn caused by a desperate economic situation, the old crisis pushed to the point of panic by the world-wide depression; that in Spain the combination of deflated currency, paralyzed industry and loss of foreign agricultural markets with huge government debts and deficits had already beaten Primo de Rivera and sent him to exile.

When the Men of the Republic walked into the echoing, undefended halls of the monarchy, they had the following problems to meet:

First, the land question. This was the picture: three-quarters of the population, dependent, directly or indirectly, on agriculture, with the land distributed and administered in such a way that not much more than 10 per cent of the agrarian population could make a decent living from it. The best, most fertile lands, concentrated in big estates, cultivated often in the most primitive and wasteful ways, sometimes even used for pastures; their owners, usually latifundists with enough land to provide incomes enabling them to support large families in Madrid or Paris.

The harshest lands, cut up into almost dooryard-size pieces, intensively worked and still usually not producing enough to feed even one family; moreover, appallingly burdened with debt. Working on the big estates, from a half million to a million landless persons, the number growing steadily; these, employed for about half the year only, at sheer subsistence wages, and the rest of the year left to migrate or steal or starve.

Second, industry. A number of large monopolies, dovetailed into the government in such a way that the budget paid for losses, the stockholders benefited from profits. Most private industry, small and medium, carrying overwhelming tax burdens; not a few of these taxes still of the feudal type, constituting what practically amounted to government toll-gates at every operation.

Third, army and bureaucracy. A federal budget supporting an enormous number of professional officers, who had already many times aroused popular hatred by sterile, costly and bloody operations in Africa; supporting also a huge bureaucracy, mainly relatives of landowners or army officers (they are all the same families), and supporting, finally, the church and its orders, which administered, as they had for five centuries, the schools, hospitals and welfare institutions, and controlled and censored most of the country's cultural life.

Fourth, an industrial proletariat enormously enlarged during the World War, now concentrated in the large cities and aroused to desperation by the triple goad of unemployment, subsistence wages and violent repression.

II

To change this picture, at the point when the Men of the Republic entered it, meant for any government, whatever its political color, immediate and radical measures. They could be measures of one of two kinds, cutting into the interests of one of the two major classes involved—the landowners, the army, the bureaucracy and the big monopolists, or the peasants, small business men and proletariat.

The former were the people who had supported Primo de Rivera and who are now represented by the Fascist generals. The latter were the ones who had voted in the republic. In the hands of the former, the government had practiced the economic dogmas of fascism: repression, wage-cutting, dissolution of labor unions, forced labor in concentration camps. The latter expected from the republic equally far-reaching measures, but of the opposite kind: government control of industries, wage-raising, redistribution of the land, rehabilitation and security projects.

But the Men of the Republic represented mixed loyalties. They were pulled in both directions, and as a result the pendulum swung for two years between measures aimed at the old ruling classes and measures of repression aimed at the mass of peasants and workers.

The swings, in turn, were determined by pressures exerted from Right and Left. The Right, which had no reason to feel it could trust a government in which there were Socialist Cabinet Ministers, froze its credits, slowed up its financial and manufacturing activities still more, paralyzed its agricultural work as much as it could, and began to employ groups of armed men to harass the Left and endanger the government.

A year and a half after April, 1931, the Right concentrated its effort on a military revolt, which occurred in the summer of 1932 and was promptly defeated, chiefly by civilian participation on the government side.

Meanwhile, on the Left, the situation of peasants and workers had not been perceptibly bettered. Growing uneasiness and dissatisfaction began to show in strikes, invasions of estates, bombings, burnings of crops. At the beginning of 1933 there was an uprising, mainly of peasants, which was put down so firmly that the government at once began to lose peasant and worker support. In that year (1933) the Socialists, pushed from Right and Left, withdrew from the Cabinet and the government was taken over by Republicans more or less closely allied with the Right, and more or less committed to its methods of economic salvation.

The result was chronic uproar, an uprising almost immediately, hundreds of strikes, and finally a nation-wide peasant strike. All of which, combined with the discovery of scandals as sensational as Teapot Dome and the Stavisky case, ended the life of that government and closed chapter two of the story of the republic.

III

Chapter three began with the attempt on the part of these rulers to hand the power over to the extreme Right, represented by Fascists, such as Gil Robles, who called themselves Republicans. This meant a still further swing and an open commitment to Fascist measures of reform and control: a farewell to democracy, with life shaped to the German and Austrian patterns. The attempt, made in the Fall of 1934, had been preceded and illustrated by the collapse of the German Republic and the battles of Fascists and Socialists in Vienna, which had made a profound impression on the common people of Spain.

For that reason mainly, the divided sectors of trades unions and labor parties had begun to come together, and chapter three of the story therefore opened with civil war. When Gil Robles was called to the Cabinet, there was a national strike, with uprisings which took several weeks to repress. The spearhead of revolt and repression was in Asturias. Here the miners, organized in united-front labor committees, took over the entire region and were dislodged only after the rest of Spain had been recaptured, and only with the use of Spain's Foreign Legion and Moorish mercenaries, a method unparalleled in the entire history of Spain.

IV

This clash gave the Left confidence and sent the pendulum swinging back. At the beginning of this year, the Left, though sore, outraged, indignant and suffering from a terrific defeat, had come together; and after a year and a quarter of strikes, martial law, street skirmishes and undercover reorganization, labor forced elections and swept the Right from power. And again, as in 1931, the masses called in the Men of the Republic.

Thus was born the Popular Front, which in fact was the same alignment as there was in 1931, except that this time there were no labor participants in the Cabinet, and most labor organizations were not enthusiastic supporters of the Republican régime. The paradox of a Republican government created by labor and resting on labor, yet exercising power not in the name of labor, was repeated, more sharply untenable than before.

The phenomenon of "dual power," that appeared in Russia during the time of Kerensky, began to make life miserable for the Men of the Republic and for the labor leaders who urged and advocated the Popular Front. This phenomenon, translated into constant struggle within every peasant and worker organization, between those who advocate taking the power directly and those who advocate letting the Republicans administer it, is the keynote of chapter four of the story of Spain's republic, which is now drawing to an end.

In the four months of its life the Popular Front government has been completely paralyzed by this struggle, and by the knowledge that the real power lodges in union headquarters. Demands from Right and Left that it take drastic measures against the other to remedy the intolerable state of economic distress have been met by small postponements, little swings repeating the swings of the first days of the republic. There has been constant battling in the streets between the armed Right and the armed Left; there have been strikes at the rate of two or three new ones a day, sometimes supported, sometimes repressed, most often ignored; political murders, and open plotting in all the armed forces of the State.

The fever-chart climbed steadily and for many weeks before July 19 it was apparent, and openly stated in most of the press, that an upheaval, provoked by a military-Fascist putsch, was imminent. Yet the government, pulled Right by the fear of Socialist revolution, pulled Left by the fear of fascism, did as in 1931: it made strong speeches and drifted.

V

And now the decisive battle has begun. It has been rehearsed on a larger and larger scale, since the fall of the monarchy and its dictatorship. Each side now knows with blinding clarity the extent of its strength, the nature of what is involved, and what will happen to it if it loses.

Each side also knows all the moves; each has fought in the streets many times before and each knows that it wins or loses according as it has the support of the common people, the great majorities of the land.

From its own history and from events in other European countries, all Spain now knows that it is launched definitively on one of two roads: fascism or socialism. It knows that the struggle to decide which is not just a question of who wins today's battles. It is something that will take months, possibly years, to decide; and the outcome depends on money as well as on arms—and almost as much on the millions of people who are not Spaniards as on the Spaniards themselves.

Part 2

THE WAR

EFFECTIVE REPORTING of the war was limited by the fact that in most of the crucial fighting neither side would permit journalists at the front. Generally speaking they had to work from official communiqués, piecing them out with brief interviews and the interpretation of rumors. Frank Kluckhohn's report on the tactics of the Moors and the Foreign Legion is exceptional in that he was able to follow operations closely during the first weeks when the Insurgents were sure that the war would be very short, and before they had become aware of a largely unfavorable world press reaction to their methods of terror. Herbert L. Matthews could report effectively on the siege of Madrid because the city itself was indeed "the front" for air and artillery operations. The short pieces on the battle of Brunete depend on the official releases in both zones, but taken together they offer quite an accurate picture of the extent of the early Republican success, the reversal brought about by counterattack, and the bloody, stalemate character of the battle as a whole. Hanson Baldwin, writing on the battle of Teruel without being an eyewitness, is nevertheless very accurate concerning the terrain, the tactics, and the psychological importance of the town to both sides. A. W. Jones, as a Quaker, was able to learn more than most foreign journalists about conditions behind the lines in both the Nationalist and Republican sectors. His article summarizes accurately and movingly the effects of hunger, air raids, and the movement of refugee populations. Finally, the entry to Barcelona is a detailed eyewitness account. The Nationalists had been uncertain whether they would meet strong resistance. Reporters were allowed to ride in with the first troops, and the article conveys vividly the sense of chaos and the expression of pent-up emotions by soldiers and civilians alike.

Death in the Afternoon —and at Dawn

by Frank L. Kluckhohn

CACARES, SPAIN.

THE NEWEST methods of warfare are blended with the oldest in this fantastically bitter Spanish civil war. There is no uniformity of action on the part of either side, Red or White, except in the ferocity with which the struggle is waged.

In one city soldiers fight hand to hand with peasants armed with knives, as in days gone by. In another, the newest of machine guns sing their rattling song of death, answered by repeating rifles. Warships exchange heavy cannonades with 8-inch shore batteries, fighting planes bomb cities and columns of troops indiscriminately.

This is guerrilla warfare with modern flourishes, and the end justifies the means at any given spot. Although both sides have an underlying plan of campaign, one often finds it hard to recognize.

Along mountain roads troops lie on their bellies shooting at snipers who harry them from the hills, or meet death under the hot sun as planes spray them with machine-gun fire. A town is taken at the point of the bayonet after barricades have been broken down; another is shelled by cannon and bombed from the air before the foreign legion enters, shouting and swearing.

On battle lines, shifting daily and often undefined, and behind the lines as well, death is meted out by women as well as men. This is more than just a war. It is a class battle, and observers who saw the Russian revolution say there is more passion in this Spanish struggle.

The insurgent forces, Rightists, have been forced to fight every step of the way through territory cut by mountain ranges and towering peaks, rising jagged against the sky. Leftist forces are prone to flee to these natural forts after losing a town, not only to save their lives but to take up a snipers' war from safe refuge.

Hence, from Seville northward, General Franco's foreign legion not only has had to capture walled cities and towns, and battle for every village along the way, but has met constant fire from the hills. Long after a district is technically "pacified" the shooting goes on behind what are euphemistically called "the lines."

This picture may seem bizarre, but it is not exaggeration to say that to get out of Spain for an hour is like passing from the nether depths to heaven. The bearded, haggard men—experienced war correspondents—who stagger across the border to send news after being under fire, feel that they have never before seen so mad a caldron as this. They are sickened by brutal murders behind the lines and by the cruelty that marks each hour of the struggle.

It is amazing, upon driving into a town, to see the bodies of twenty executed persons just outside and then to turn a corner and catch sight of a young man and a girl courting. It is fantastic to find a motion-picture show going on in a bullet-scarred theatre as a bombing plane soars menacingly overhead; or to pass along a calm road for forty miles and then have bullets rip into your car.

Here is a bull ring where, several weeks ago, crowds saw men play with death. Now the crowds are meeting death here themselves. The volleys crack—never even: first one shot, then a series, then another series. At 5 in the afternoon, at 2 in the morning, at dawn. Four thousand died at Badajoz.

The sound of these executions and their meaning sink down into the marrow of those who hear them. It is a reign of fear that begets fear. The sympathizers of Soldier Pablo know that, if the tide of war turns, Red José will kill them in the same way. Marcial's brother has been executed in Barcelona, and Marcial is mad to get there to shoot some of those who did his brother in. Each of these represents thousands of his fellows.

Two motor cars filled with Reds drive down the road. The occupants see a guard across the way with rifles, take them for fellow-Reds, stop to show their safe conduct papers—and realize their mistake too late. They clamber out and start to run. Shots drop them, mortally wounded. They beg to be put out of pain.

"Talk, then, about your forces," they are told. They mumble.

"If you know so much, you must know more," their captors say.

Finally, after an hour or two, they die, victims of a war that knows no fixed front or rear, no distinction between men and women, between combatants and noncombatants.

The medieval-walled cities have been hard nuts for even the best troops to crack. These cities were constructed to meet the shock of ancient war; their walls, twenty feet thick, withstand even the modern cannon. It is through the gates, often after hours of withering fire on both sides, that entry must be made.

Even those towns and villages which are not Middle-Age strongholds are often built in an unbroken circle, with the back walls of whitewashed homes facing outward. Thus a force of, say, a hundred men and women can hold these villages for hours against superior numbers of trained troops equipped with machine guns and cannon. The struggle for almost every hamlet is fierce.

In a military sense, Spain's excellent system of paved roads makes it easier to wage this war. The transportation of troops is relatively easy. And, thanks to the American-constructed telephone system that reaches almost every village, each military headquarters knows from minute to minute what is going on in its territory.

An anecdote is told of a Moor who picked up a ringing telephone after the Rebels captured Telavera, on the road to Madrid. He heard a voice say, "This is the Minister of War in Madrid. How is everything going?"

"Well, if you really want to know, we Moors just took the

town," was the reply, as the white-turbaned Arab threw the telephone on the floor and ran to tell his brethren he had spoken "over the air." At any rate, news does get around fast.

Picturesque, indeed, are the troops of both sides. As far as the Left force is concerned, the "Marxist" militia forms the backbone of the government's defense. Unfortunately for offensive plans, these militia men and girls are still largely an undisciplined lot. Some bands are Socialist, some Anarchist, each group is eager to outdo the other and each is reluctant to obey orders from anyone.

A Red militiaman, captured by the insurgents and condemned to death, was asked by his captors what he did as a soldier.

"Sometimes what I am told; sometimes what I wish," was the reply. He was led off and shot.

Some of these volunteers are dressed in khaki uniforms with overseas caps, others just don blue denim, put on cloth-soled sandals and let it go at that. They fight fiercely on the defensive and outnumber their opponents heavily. It is difficult to dislodge them from entrenched positions—perhaps because they know what happens to those who surrender.

A large percentage of those ready fighters in patent-leather hats and olive-green uniforms, the Civil Guards, also fight under Leftist orders. The radicals count, too, upon thousands of blue-clad assault guards, members of a police force created by the five-year-old republic, and upon some regular conscript troops within their territory.

Against these overwhelming numbers the Rightists have perhaps 30,000 trained troops—a good part of Spain's conscript army—and the Moors, foreign legion and Moroccan regulars, who are the spearhead of attacks on all fronts.

Behind the lines these Moors loll on their sides in the streets of villages, their baggy tan trousers grimy, their fezes or turbans askew, as they laugh and joke among themselves. They look as though they would be too undisciplined to be much good under fire.

In action, particularly when they are facing deadly shooting, they are cool, self-possessed and passionless. They obey orders implicitly and fire with a precision unusual in this war. They believe that in war they have a right to loot, and their passion is for manufactured implements that they do not understand. Radio sets are their particular looting pets.

A column of these Arabs is advancing up a road under the command of Spanish officers. Two Red war planes appear as specks in the sky, draw nearer.

They disperse behind olive trees, their guns ready. The planes zip by not far off the ground, their machine guns spitting. Several Moors fire back. The performance is repeated. Then the planes disappear in the distance.

"Fall in!" shouts an officer.

Meekly and calmly they continue their march. Soon they will be fighting again, with the same calm deliberation.

Quite different is the foreign legion, sprinkled with men of American, British, German and even Chinese extraction, but made up mainly of Spanish mercenaries. This outfit is tough and vicious. When the legion attacks, it goes forward angry and muttering, lifted above itself by the fierce desire for combat and hatred for its opponents. It does not like to be stopped.

The Moroccan regulars consist largely of Spaniards of much the same caliber, but with somewhat less esprit de corps. The conscripts commanded by General Mola in the north are poorly trained and much less effective than any of the three organizations mentioned.

In brief, it may be said that, as far as military action is concerned, this is a war of a very small body of trained troops against a vastly superior number of unorganized opponents aided by natural obstacles.

Perhaps even more than in the Ethiopian war, airplanes have proved exceedingly effective. In the early days of the revolution Red planes played a big part in checking General Mola's advance from the north on Madrid. German and Italian planes, manned by Germans and Italians, later put the insurgents in a better position.

General Franco has been able to carry out, under real war conditions, the long-discussed experiment of moving troops across enemy territory to fight. He not only brought much of his fighting force across from Morocco by air, but sent troops across Red territory to relieve beleaguered Rightist Granada. From Granada factories he brought out by plane dynamite needed for military purposes.

Airplanes have also proved useful in cracking civilian morale. The persistent bombing of cities and towns by both sides has had a greater moral effect, though actual damage has been slight.

Against warships the planes have not done so well, though the Leftist battleship Jaime I was put out of commission for several critical weeks by bombs dropped as she lay in dock. War planes were able, at least once, to engage Leftist ships at sea, making it possible for General Franco to bring a convoy of troops by water from Morocco.

It was when General Franco got these thousands of soldiers to Spain that the military adventure, which was slowly collapsing in the south and stalled in the north, became a reborn movement. It was then that the broad plans of White and Red strategy were born. With a picture of the conditions of warfare, implements and men engaged, it is fairly simple to trace the plans.

Diminutive Franco found the territory held by his forces spotted with red. The Reds controlled Madrid and the entire east coast of Spain, as well as of the northern ports. Granada, held by a handful of White troops, was cut off from White headquarters at Seville.

The White generalissimo thereupon sent General Varela off to relieve Granada and threaten Malaga, which with 30,000 armed Reds threatened the rear of his southern army. He ordered General Mola to take the north coast cities and eliminate the danger from the northern rear, and sent most of his picked troops off for Toledo and Madrid.

The tactics used in carrying out the Whites' plan of campaign have been as unusual as the conditions that made them necessary. The fact that civilians acted as combatants wherever the military advanced made the creation of "flying" columns necessary.

Groups of some 300 soldiers each have been loaded into trucks and sent out in cavalcades to capture recalcitrant towns off the main roads, thus reducing the danger of attacks on communication lines. On occasion General Franco has had from thirty to forty of these columns operating simultaneously, assisted by Rebel bombing planes.

In his advance toward Madrid, at various times he has split his troops up into three columns, all moving toward their goal along parallel roads and fighting through every town reached and frequently along the roads.

Whenever a town is taken, Rightist militia, uniformed in blue denim, assume control and permit the military to move on to new objectives. These volunteers, while of small use in the firing line, are all armed, and outnumber the actual fighting forces by at least three to one. They are responsible for preventing disorders in the places conquered and they perform most of the summary executions.

The Leftists have followed an entirely different strategy. They have gone on the assumption that the longer the revolt continues, the greater the chance of its collapsing behind the lines. Their leaders believe that the reasonably large percentage of the people who are accepting the military only because of terrorist tactics will rise up if the struggle goes on long enough.

Attempts have been made by Red agents to stir up revolt among the tribes in White Morocco. Enough progress has been made to stop the movement of troops to Spain in any large numbers. The Red leaders insist that, even if the Whites can take small towns and isolated north coast cities, this constitutes no assurance that they can win the war. Even with Madrid in Rebel hands, they believe, the armed peasants would still be out in the hills and mountains, and a large part of Spain would remain in Leftist hands.

Under the Death-spurting Skies of War-torn Madrid

by Herbert L. Matthews

MADRID.

THERE ARE six-story houses in the Rosales district, on the western edge of Madrid, where 100-kilo bombs have plowed right through and into the ground, exposing parts of rooms on each floor. It is like a strange and horrible stage scene where the fourth wall is nonexistent so that the characters can present a tragedy before an unseen audience. If one were to cut down like that through life in Madrid under the siege, what could be seen?

The nonchalance of these people is staggering to behold. One would think that all their lives they had lived amid the booming of cannons, the explosions of shells and the rending crashes of aerial bombs. They seem to possess a sense that is almost animal-like in its egoism. There is surely no people in the world who circumscribe their lives so tightly as the Spaniards. Their individualism has something primitive about it. You have to go back through the historic stages of society, through nations, city-states and even tribes, to the dawn of social life, when only the family mattered. To touch a Spaniard to the quick you have to strike at him personally, at his family and his private possessions.

Walk up the Alcalá some afternoon when the Gran Via, just to your right, is being heavily shelled, as it often has been in the past three months. You would look in vain on the faces of the people strolling up and down for any appreciation of the fact that death and havoc are within 100 yards or so of them. The crash of a shell might induce the men to interrupt their conversation for a passing comment. The women go on with their shopping, the children with their play. What is there to get excited about? The shelling is 100 yards away!

They will not believe that the next shell might indeed interrupt conversation and shopping and play. Obviously, such a thing is inconceivable.

There is a building in town that has been shelled many times. Usually the shelling has taken place between 4 and 5 in the afternoon. The block of sidewalk that runs before its façade is the most dangerous spot in town. Those of us newspaper men who have to pass it four or five times a day do so at a walk that is half a run, and we breathe a sigh of relief as we duck around the corner. Yet how often in our haste do we pass children spinning tops on that very sidewalk, while their mothers look on complacently!

During a bombardment militiamen work like Trojans in their efforts to stop people from crossing in front of the building—but quite unsuccessfully. One would expect that passers-by, who could take any number of side streets, would give the spot a wide berth. Not the Madrileños! A shell bursts and the street is cleared as if by magic; a minute later people are bustling by again, pointing excitedly at the damage which the last shell has done.

If you stopped them and called attention to the fact that the next shell might be labeled with their names, they would doubtless look at you in astonishment. It is the other fellow who is going to be killed, not they! The imagination which could substitute for fear and prudence is lacking. The Spaniard is a realist: he is alive, strong, well. These are facts, palpable facts. The conception of himself blown to bits is a figment of the imagination. And so he politely walks on.

Winter is nasty in Madrid. There are sudden shifts in temperature and the cold is peculiarly penetrating, particularly that proverbial wind from the Guadarramas which will kill a man but will not extinguish a candle. This year there has been an unusual amount of rain and fog. Coal is scarce. The railroads into Madrid have been cut for nearly three months. Truck trains must concentrate on bringing only the necessaries of life and war materials.

There are ways of keeping warm without steam heat or blazing fireplaces, but you cannot cook food without something to heat your stove. And so there is an incessant search for wood—any kind of wood.

A bomb landed in a square off the Castellana a few weeks ago. Several people were killed and a half-dozen wounded. From the Telefonica a few of us had spotted the location and we rushed down there to see what had happened. Ambulances were just taking away the dead and wounded. A man with a hastily bandaged head was being led off by some friends. But it was not that which caught our astonished attention. A tree had been blown down by the explosion and at least ten people were hacking furiously away at the trunk and branches. In a quarter of an hour nothing was left but a short stump where the trunk had broken off, and a boy was chopping at it diligently, as close to the ground as he could get, so that none of that precious fuel would be lost.

In Rosales, in Arguelles, in Tetuan—the districts of Madrid that have been most heavily bombed—it is a common sight to see men, women and children foraging among the ruins of houses for parts of beams, pieces of flooring, broken furniture—anything so long as it is wood and will burn. At a time when Rosales was a death trap the authorities tried to discourage the practice by forcing people to give up the wood they collected, but others came and it was hopeless.

A few days ago when a building in the center of the town was being shelled heavily with eight-inch high explosives the wooden slats of half a dozen shutters were blown into the street. It was a no man's land—or it should have been—yet that did not deter two stout housekeepers from dashing across the street and tucking as much of the wood as they could hold under their arms. The shells were hitting at about three-minute intervals, but the opportunity was too precious. They lingered a few seconds longer than they should have, for as they bustled back across the street the next shell crashed into the building, sending down a shower of stones and glass. Somehow they escaped; somehow they scooted over the ground at a pace that fleet young maidens could not have equaled, and off they went with their wood—genuine spoils of war.

Five minutes later I saw a 10-year-old boy on the same spot hastily gathering what was left. He ran around the corner and out of sight just as a shell roared into the edifice at the top, above where he must have been. In my dispatch that day I cabled: "He is a lucky youngster if he escaped the falling stones and bricks and the flying glass that spray the street at such moments." The following day I learned that he had been killed.

In the restaurant where I eat lunch nearly every day, Sebastian, the head waiter, invariably presents a complicated menu with due suavity and seriousness. One's eye passes sadly across the long lists of fish, meat, fowl, cheeses, desserts, and, finally, having reached the end of the printed part, alights on a few miserable lines written in ink. "What will you have today?" asks Sebastian, no doubt from force of habit. As if there were a choice! All that the menu offers is rice cooked in rancid olive oil, a thin slice of beef, breaded and fried in the same oil, and oranges—just that and nothing more, day after day, week after week. And Sebastian runs the best restaurant in town!

That is very natural, of course. Wartime, anywhere, is a time for tightening the belt—above all in a city under siege. No one is starving here, and no one is going to starve, but these are lean days, and Madrid is a hungry city. That is why, when newcomers first arrive in the capital, the feature of daily life which strikes them above all is the food queue. Queues are everywhere; you cannot walk three blocks in any part of town during the morning without seeing long lines of women. Sometimes it is to buy a few pounds of dried olive seeds to use as fuel; sometimes it is for oil, sometimes for rice or cauliflowers or oranges.

Women wait hours in the cold, perhaps all morning. Those at the end of the queue might well find supplies exhausted before they arrive, yet the astonishing thing about those lines is the good humor with which the women wait. There are never any complaints, never any sad or disgruntled faces. They gossip and laugh and build themselves little fires, if there is any refuse around, and somehow the time passes.

Now and then carts will drive into town, perhaps with a load of cabbages. It makes a triumphal procession, for housekeepers and even passers-by, seeing it, will follow doggedly to the stopping place—and then the line is already made and the sale begins.

It takes fortitude and high spirits to do that sort of thing, week after week, and still keep on smiling—but the Madrileñas are doing it, and more. Those lines are there when the bombers come over and when the shells fly—and they are still there afterward. In Tetuan a few weeks ago an Insurgent pursuit plane swooped down low over a main street where there was a long queue of women before a grocer's shop. At a cruelly precise moment the machine gunner let go full blast straight into the petrified group of housekeepers. Some twelve or fourteen were killed or wounded.

I arrived on the scene about twenty minutes later. The bodies had been taken away to the morgue, the wounded to a hospital. And then the line had re-formed! I should never have noticed anything wrong if it had not been for the blood on the street, which caught my attention and set me to asking questions. They talked excitedly, bitterly, but obviously the idea of giving up their places in line or foregoing their purchases never occurred to any of them.

Suppose some autocratic power were to say to the inhabitants of New York City: "Tonight, and every night hereafter for weeks and months, the city must remain in total darkness. None of you may leave your homes after 10 o'clock. No restaurants may be open for dinner—no movies, no theatres, no cabarets, no bars. Your houses and apartments must not show a gleam of light. Although it is Winter, they will not be heated. And sleep if you can, for outside you will hear the boom of cannon all night, and perhaps the roar of enemy planes carrying death and destruction to you and your loved ones."

"Inconceivable!" the reader will say. But that is exactly what has happened to Madrid. I am writing this at night in my room at the American Embassy. The outer and inner shutters of the window are tightly closed so that no light shows in the street. A blanket is wrapped around me for warmth. Outside, the dull thud of cannonading in University City is echoed back to me from a big building across the Castellana. And how do I know that tonight Insurgent bombers, which have already narrowly missed the embassy twice, will not come over again?

There are no gay white ways in Madrid under the siege. The Gran Via, where fashionable crowds were wont to stroll at night while stores and cafés, restaurants and theatres blazed with light, now dies an unnatural death when night falls. By 6 o'clock everything is dark and the crowds rushing home from work seem like ghosts flitting through an unreal world. By 9 the bustle has disappeared and guards commence to look askance at each passer-by. From 10 o'clock on it is a city of the dead, and woe betide any one found walking abroad without the password or proper documents. Even people, like newspaper men, who have the run of the city at night, who get the password and have all the documents necessary, go out no oftener than is absolutely necessary—which is, perhaps, a few times a week.

There is no danger for them now, but theirs is a very uncomfortable sensation. Between here and the Telefonica, a twenty-minute walk, one is challenged four or five times by unseen guards. The street is so dark that you cannot see where you are putting your feet. You purposely walk heavily, talk loudly and puff incessantly at your cigarette, so that the guards will have full warning of your coming and not see lurking Fascists in your presumably stealthy approach. Then you strain your ears for the guard's quiet, but oh! so imperative, "Alto!" You stand rooted to the spot while he approaches and either gives his half of the password or asks to see your documents. Then, with a courteous apology for having bothered you and a hearty "Salud!" he lets you go.

In the confusion of the early weeks of the war it was not so safe, or so courteous, a process, but patrolling is now in the hands of the Assault Guards, who are a genuine protection for those with business abroad.

One night a group of British correspondents were returning to their embassy about midnight. They had neglected to get the password, which frequently saves the inconvenience of showing documents but is generally not necessary. That night the guards asked: "A donde vamos?" (Where are we going?), and the answer was: "A vencer." (To victory.)

With their documents the group had no trouble so far as the first few patrols were concerned. But at the third they heard a guard call out: "Halt! Where are we going?"

"To the British Embassy," they replied.

They were wrong: they went to jail, although not for the whole night.

Of course, war has its bright side as well as its dark. The "vin ordinaire," or table wine, disappeared very quickly in and around Madrid. So Tom, Dick and Harry, whose palates never knew the taste of vintage wine before, are drinking from bottles that now-missing tourists would have smacked their lips over. In a hotel at the Escorial a few weeks ago I had a lunch that was graced with a bottle of white Tondonia, 1918.

There are no more cheap cigars left? All right, we will smoke Coronas, Hoyo de Montereys, Partagas, and even rarer brands. As time goes on the cigars get better. Two months ago when I first arrived in Madrid it was still possible to get Havana cigars at 90 centimes, or 1 peseta, but now they have been exhausted, and the 1.50 peseta cigars are almost gone, too. So we are starting to smoke 2 and 2.50 peseta cigars—and that goes for militiamen as well as foreigners. And it is worth noting that a Corona Corona, for instance, at 2.75 pesetas is one-third the price that has to be paid in New York at the present rate of the peseta.

Among the first things to be requisitioned for war purposes were the automobiles. Some got Fords, Opels, Citroëns of ancient vintage, but many got Hispano-Suizas, Rolls-Royces and Chryslers of the latest model. For a man who can ride in a Mercedes limousine and smoke a Magnolia Havana this is not such a bad war after all.

And then there were the fashionable apartments and palaces. The aristocracy has been driven away, and, with the need for housing, their homes had to be used. Political and syndical organizations took over most of the palaces. Refugees have swarmed in from outlying towns, and they had to be housed somewhere, so why not put them in the expensively furnished apartments of this or that grandee and industrialist?

Many thousands of poor people who never knew anything but the starkest sort of poverty have now learned how the other half lived. Will they ever be content again to return to their poverty?

"Why is it," I asked a guard after the bombing of Jan. 20, "that all the casualties today were women and children?"

It was something that had often puzzled me in the last two months. The victims were not always women and children, but at least these always far outnumbered the men victims.

Then he told me what he had seen with his own eyes that morning. The bombers roared out of a mist only ten seconds before the fatal moment for releasing missiles. There was no time to be lost, no time even to run for a refuge. There is only one thing to be done in a case like that—throw yourself face downward on the ground and place your hands on the back of your head. A bomb explodes upward, and unless it lands on top of you, or very close, your chances of escape are excellent, if you do that.

That morning the thing which had to be done was very obvious. The men did it, and were flat on the ground with seconds to spare. Not so the women or the children. The latter, of course, did not know any better. For them there was only the universal law: terrified, they ran toward their mothers, or else, panic-stricken, they stood wide-eyed and still. Spanish mothers are not different from any others. It was their children they thought of, not themselves. And so they rushed toward them, blindly, instinctively, as if a mother's bosom were protection against 100-kilo bombs.

The ten seconds passed. Fifteen killed, sixteen wounded—all women and children!

Madrid has lately been plastered with posters exhorting, begging, ordering non-combatants to evacuate Madrid. One of them shows a huge bomb, larger than the apartment houses it is smashing at the bottom of the picture. The conception is valid. In power they are greater than buildings, far greater than those six-story houses in the Rosales district, where parts of rooms on each floor are now exposed, like the scenes of a stage.

The Battle of Brunete

GREAT OPEN BATTLE IN VIEW AS GOVERNMENT ADDS TO GAINS

By Herbert L. Matthews

MADRID, JULY 11 [1937].

SPANISH GOVERNMENT troops early today occupied Villanueva del Pardillo, about twelve miles west of Madrid, and took 600 more prisoners. This operation widened their salient and carried one step further the greatest government offensive of the civil war.

Since Monday the Loyalist forces have been making wide gains in a supreme effort to break the siege of Madrid, and this drive is regarded here as even stronger than the Rebel offensive against Bilbao. It is, therefore, no exaggeration to say that the war has reached its most crucial period.

It is hoped by the Loyalists that the race against time that the Negrin Government lost in the case of Bilbao will be won for Santander and Asturias.

In less than two months the government has worked a complete reorganization of the army and air forces, speeded up the war industries, made heavy purchases abroad and built up a great fighting machine. For weeks men, guns and materials of all sorts have been pouring up, choking roads with thousands of trucks. Planes by the dozens are filling the air over the Rebel lines, bombing towns, concentrations and trenches at will and again demonstrating that in Central Spain the Loyalists still dominate the air.

Equipment Is Extensive

Details of equipment cannot, of course, be given, but it can be said that there are many tanks, many guns and more troops than have yet been employed in this conflict.

The government is playing for the greatest of stakes, since, if it wins, the siege of Madrid will have been lifted. It is too soon to make any predictions. The Insurgents are naturally preparing a counter-offensive and, since the action is now in open territory, one must suppose that the first great open battle of the war will occur soon.

The offensive, whose first phase has ended with the capture of Villanueva del Pardillo, is conceded by foreign military experts here to be of particularly brilliant conception. Apparently the whole general staff worked it out, and those of us who have been watching its development see no reason to doubt that its direction has been entrusted to two Spanish officers—General José Miaja and Lieut. Col. Vicente Rojo, chief of the general staff.

The plan of campaign was and still is an intricate one. Its first part was successfully kept secret until it was launched, and its further development remains a mystery, except that it can clearly be seen from the map that the main thrust is in the direction of Navalcarnero, eighteen miles southwest of Madrid, and presumably intended to cut the Estremadura Road, which would automatically make the withdrawal of all Rebel forces around Madrid a virtual necessity, for that is the Insurgents' main line of communication. There is no necessity to save Navalcarnero itself and there is no reason to suppose that the Loyalists intend to waste troops yet to try to do so.

It was at dawn last Monday that the offensive began, with a feint up from Aranjuez, twenty-eight miles southeast of Madrid, toward Sesena. The Rebels, of course, had known that an offensive was coming and General Gonzalo Queipo de Llano had even shouted jovially into the Seville radio a few nights earlier something to this effect: "Bring on your old offensive; we are ready for you."

Events proved, however, that the Insurgents had not known just where the drive was coming from, when it was going to start and how powerful it was going to be. That was one of the reasons that foreign correspondents were not allowed to give anything more than the harmless communiqué of Monday night saying that an offensive action had been initiated against Sesena.

It was at dawn Tuesday that the government really showed its hand, and before the Loyalists could be stopped they had won their greatest victory since Brihuega in the capture of Brunete.

Start of Loyalist Thrust

The start of the government's main thrust was at Valdemorillo, on what is being referred to as the Sierra front. The Rebel positions were based upon the fortified towns of Navalagamella, Quijorna, Villanueva de la Cañada and Villanueva del Pardillo.

There was no trench system along there, for no fighting had occurred in that sector. From every viewpoint it was, in fact, the best possible point that could have been chosen for an offensive.

Moreover, the Loyalists cleverly avoided those fortified towns first and simply drove through open country down the valley of the Guadarrama River, keeping to the western bank. That safeguarded their left flank.

It was a brigade of the Fifth Corps to which was assigned the objective of Brunete, an important town that stands at crossroads leading to Madrid, El Escorial, Navalcarnero and San Martin de Valdeiglesias. They were ordered to take it by noon.

At 8 o'clock in the morning they were in possession of it and by noon they had advised headquarters that they had dug in and fortified their positions. That alone showed how the Rebels were caught napping, for Brunete was not defended.

Meanwhile, the air force had been putting on a terrific display of strength. Every single Rebel town in that whole territory was severely bombed, including the Insurgent headquarters at Navalcarnero.

Scant Rebel Resistance

Only once during the day did the Rebel air force make a serious attempt to stop the Loyalist fliers. That was over Navalcarnero late in the afternoon when ten Heinkel fighters attacked the government planes. Two of them were shot down.

In driving on Brunete the Loyalists had passed between Villanueva de la Cañada and Quijorna, but it was imperative to take those towns, for otherwise Brunete could not be held.

To American volunteers go the chief honors for storming Villanueva de la Cañada, and it was a hard fight that lasted from early afternoon until 10 P. M. Quijorna also had been completely surrounded, but it put up a still harder battle and it was not taken until 11:30 Friday morning.

On Wednesday another feint had been made south of the Tagus, where a village was taken, while the Third Army Corps struck again toward Sesena.

On that day Insurgent planes brought down from the Santander sector began offering fiercer resistance. Fiat two-seater fighters were used for the first time on the central front and a Loyalist aviator told me admiringly that they were fine planes and were being courageously handled.

However, the Government air force again succeeded in bombing and strafing dozens of objectives all through the terrain.

FRANCO SAYS DRIVE OF FOE IS A FAILURE

By William P. Carney

SALAMANCA, SPAIN, JULY 14.

GENERAL FRANCISCO FRANCO announced that the enemy's offensive on the Madrid front already had ended in complete failure when he received the foreign press correspondents today in his general headquarters.

"All of you can go to the front now and verify personally that the heavy fighting is over. You won't see any great battles, because our forces today are engaged in merely straightening out the lines which withstood the powerful assault launched by the enemy eight days ago with a large number of effectives and supported by a tremendous amount of war material and aviation strength.

"I am glad to welcome you here, and I wish to thank you for your work with us, particularly because we have no money for propaganda. You are free to go wherever you like. We only ask you to tell the truth. You will find order everywhere and life as normal as it can be in war times.

"Our movement is based on order and justice. Truth is our principal ally and at the front you can see the truly wonderful spirit of our troops. I hope you can all visit Spain after we have won our victory, so you can see what our country is like in peacetime. We want your countries to know and understand Spain."

Fifty-seven enemy planes were brought down during the eight days of activity in the Brunete sector, while the Nationalists [Rebels] lost only five machines, according to the "verified" figures given in an official communiqué at general headquarters, which added that twelve other enemy planes "probably were shot down, but positive information concerning them is not available." Eight enemy machines were grounded yesterday, it was said, and among the six pilots who bailed out and were captured five were Russian and one American.

Lieut. Col. Antonio Barroso of the Insurgent general staff today revealed the actual positions of the contending forces on the Madrid front, in addition to some outstanding results of the fighting there during the last seven days. His "conservative estimate" of the government's casualties was 12,000, of which 2,300 dead were counted by Insurgent officers in various battle sectors.

"This major offensive intended to drive us back from the gates of Madrid seems about to be liquidated decisively," Colonel Barroso stated. "We may soon also resume our big push on Santander. From Escorial and above El Pardo the Reds [Loyalists] attacked a week ago today with 30,000 men, 99 planes and 160 Russian tanks.

"Their right wing advanced rapidly through Quijorna and Villanueva de la Cañada, while the left wing pushed through Las Rozas. The wings converged at Brunete, where we stopped them.

"Another enemy force tried to swing through Carabanchel and Villaverde over to Mostoles on the Estremadura road, where they hoped to join those coming from Brunete, but this drive was halted at Carabanchel. They never captured Sevilla la Nueva, Villaviciosa, Boadilla, Aravaca, Pozuelo or El Plantio on the Corunna highway, as they claimed in their radio communiqués. They are now trying to battle their way out of a triangular pocket within the three points of Las Rozas, Brunete and Escorial.

"Picked forces from the International Brigades, including the Lister and Fourteenth Battalions, engaged in the heaviest part of the fighting. There was extensive artillery preparation for the initial attacks and I believe the cooperation of fifty-one pursuit planes and forty-eight bombers, an air force unequaled in any single operation during the World War.

"On the second day of the offensive the Reds attacked with three squadrons of cavalry and in the open country which afforded no shelter, and our aviation was well able to cut them to pieces. Our fliers also shot down twenty-six planes up to last night. The Russian tanks did not prove to be a formidable war engine. They are fast and have a quick firing two-inch gun mounted on a revolving turret which shoots two kinds of shells, one perforating and the other explosive. But a hand grenade or a bottle of inflammable liquid thrown into the caterpillar tread can completely disable them.

"We captured a great many."

LOYALIST ADVANCE CONTINUES

By Herbert L. Matthews

MADRID, JULY 14.

THE LOYALIST ADVANCE in the Sierra sector "proceeded" today according to a communiqué tonight, but evidently no new town was taken or lost. Correspondents have not been allowed to go to the front since this offensive began.

The air force did not have a good day, losing two planes to none for the Rebels, according to an official communiqué. The air activity remains intense, with a great deal of bombing on both sides out at the front. Today the Loyalists concentrated on Majadahonda and Villafranca del Castillo just off the Escorial road.

The first phase of the offensive, as the writer stated several days ago, is now over. With the taking of Villanueva del Pardillo the entire salient on the Escorial road down below Brunete was cleared, occupied and fortified.

It took eight days and ended with the original troops in a state of exhaustion, as was natural. An American soldier to whom I spoke today told of one moment yesterday when he and his comrades, standing wearily in a trench they had just dug, saw a group of Moors within easy shooting distance but were so tired they did not feel capable of raising their guns and firing with any degree of accuracy.

Those troops have done their job and done it well. Now every one is waiting for the next phase of the offensive, for it is certain that the government has not by any means unleashed more than part of its strength. We have all seen enough of the men and materials available to know that much, without receiving confirmation from the men returning from the front. What amounts to a complicated campaign now is under way and only the beginning of it has been seen so far.

REBELS IN BRUNETE AFTER HARD BATTLE

By Herbert L. Matthews

MADRID, JULY 24.

BRUNETE CHANGED HANDS today in a series of smashing attacks and counterattacks that first drove the Loyalists completely out of their positions and then after dark carried them back into the important town on the southern tip of the government's new salient. The Insurgents still retained part of it.

All accounts agree the fight, which continued without a lull from dawn into the night, was terrific. Even an official communiqué issued while the struggle inside the town was still going on speaks of its "enormous violence."

The initial drive of the Insurgents this morning, after tremendous aerial and artillery preparation, was obviously overwhelming. The Eleventh Loyalist Division was blasted right out of its positions and had to abandon Brunete. Then tanks came over and finally ground troops.

Insurgents Dug In

As the Insurgents feverishly dug in, the Loyalists prepared for a counterattack, which was carried out in the afternoon by the Fourteenth Division, covered by tanks and artillery and aided by the Eleventh Division and other forces of the same army corps.

That drive carried the government troops right up to the southeastern edge of Brunete. There they got what amounted to a toehold, to which they clung grimly for several hours. Then late in the afternoon they surged forward again, this time gaining possession of part of the town.

After night fell a bitter struggle went on for house after house, and by 9 o'clock the Loyalists were once again holding much of the town.

This has been a day of extremely heavy casualties on both sides. According to official accounts, there has been recklessness in this attack and in last Sunday's counter-offensive, which has not been equalled in the war. Correspondents have not been allowed to go to the front, and it can only be said that, if the version of the news we are receiving here is true, this relatively fruitless Rebel counter-offensive may represent one of the war's most serious setbacks for General Francisco Franco.

First Raid Repelled

The first raid apparently was thrust back without the loss of any government terrain. It appears, in fact, to have been a definite

defeat for the Rebels, since not those first troops but fresh reinforcements were thrown forward in the second attack early in the
afternoon.

Officers returning from the front said the Insurgents came on in
mass formation, despite withering machine-gun fire. Moreover,
they sent wave after wave against the Loyalist lines.

Meanwhile momentary aerial domination, gained by the element
of surprise this morning, was lost this afternoon as Loyalist planes
engaged the Rebels over the battlefield.

Details of the fighting stressed its intensity. Moreover, it appears
the first impetus of their drive carried the Insurgents to the edge
of Brunete, although evidently at a heavy cost. Some of their
units were said to have lost half their men.

Then government troops counterattacked, regaining their original positions and even slightly bettering them at some points. In
their charges the Insurgents, it is stated, had to leave their wounded
on the field, and these were taken prisoner. Most of them were
said to be Moors.

On the Sierra front it is only towns that are of prime importance
as there are no trench systems between them.

[By the *Associated Press*]

Brunete Is Key to Salient

MADRID, JULY 24

Brunete is the pivotal town in this campaign, fifteen miles west of
Madrid. If the Insurgents can dislodge General José Miaja's strong
force there, they may defeat the government's attempt to lift the
siege of Madrid. Collapse of the government offensive might turn
the war decisively in the Insurgents' favor.

Brunete is the tip of the government's southward-pointing salient. Its loss would endanger the whole salient and the men and
munitions General Miaja's troops have massed inside. A successful
government advance from Brunete would aim at Navalcarnero,
the Insurgents' supply and communication base for the siege.

The Insurgent supply road from Navalcarnero to Brunete was

heavily shelled and bombed from the air because of reports that Insurgents had been accumulating large stores of munitions and cannon along it. Government officers said the bombardments also struck heavy Insurgent troop reinforcements moving up from Navalcarnero.

Six government airplanes bombed the Usera and Villaverde sectors of the siege line south of Madrid. The explosions in Insurgent positions could be seen from roof-tops in the capital, followed by bursts of machine-gun and rifle fire.

Six persons were reported killed and twenty wounded in a heavy Insurgent air raid on Tortosa in Eastern Spain.

Franco Reports Success

HENDAYE, FRANCE, JULY 24

General Francisco Franco's war communiqué today said the Insurgents were pushing the advance to "beat down the last resistance of the enemy" west of Madrid.

Caceres, capital of the province of that name and deep within Insurgent territory in Southwestern Spain, was reported by General Franco's headquarters to have been bombed, with the loss of several lives. The Insurgent chieftain warned the Madrid-Valencia government that attacks on towns behind the front lines would bring "prompt reprisals such as we have already made."

Insurgents declared that as a result of their "recent victories" government troops able to take part in the fighting were reduced by from 15,000 to 40,000.

Taking of Teruel Upsets Prophecies

by Hanson W. Baldwin

MANUEL AZAÑA, President of the third of Spain controlled by government forces, declared last week that the capture of Teruel "had changed the face" of the Spanish civil war. And, unlike many official statements coming from either side in "Europe's undeclared war," this claim was not hyperbole. The successful surprise attack of the government upon the mountain village of Teruel, principal town in an Insurgent salient jutting toward Valencia, was something of a material victory for government arms and considerably more of a moral one.

Only a brief time ago world opinion was convinced of the inevitability of an Insurgent triumph, which was to come a few months hence. The armies of Generalissimo Francisco Franco were poised, according to repeated and insistent reports, for an offensive designed to smash through the government defenses, probably on the Aragon front, and pave the way for final victory. But the Loyalists struck before Franco. The capture of Teruel, while representing no great military achievement, gave the tonic of victory to the government's war-weary troops and people, and was important also because of its effect upon opinion outside Spain.

Eighteen Months of War

In order properly to evaluate the significance of the fight at Teruel in the history of the war it is necessary to review briefly the course the war has taken and to estimate the strengths of the forces now locked in combat along a 750-mile front.

The war started in July, 1936, with simultaneous uprisings in Morocco and in many parts of Spain. It was evident that the rebellion had been carefully planned, with the aim of quickly replacing the government with an administration headed by General Franco and probably modeled on the government of the totalitarian states.

Morocco swiftly became Franco's; so did Seville, Salamanca, Burgos, a large part of the French border region, most of Andalusia and the area around Gibraltar. Most of the Spanish Army and a sizable portion of the Navy, including practically all officers who were not slain or captured by crews who refused to join the revolt, followed the star of Franco—north toward Madrid, eastward toward Catalonia and Valencia, and toward that Mediterranean section of Spain which put down the revolution.

Franco's Advantages

Franco controlled most of the trained manpower of Spain, many of the important arsenals and raw material centers, and the great recruiting ground of Morocco. Of particular importance, he early assumed virtual control of the sea and superiority in the air.

The early weeks of the conflict were marked not only by the excesses that war always engenders but also by heroic bravery and conspicuous endurance on both sides.

Franco reached the outskirts of Madrid more than a year ago; the Loyalist armies, more a disorganized rabble of armed men than an army, were seemingly beaten. But the Insurgent leader hesitated, and the golden opportunity was lost. International brigades of volunteers, raw to the rifle and green to command, were rushed into the Loyalist front lines, supported by Russian aid; but in turn Italian and German help, in the form of men and machines of war and probably money or credits, bolstered materially and significantly the armies of Franco. The Spanish Civil War quickly became, in miniature, a European war.

Insurgent Victories

Franco, though checked at the gates of Madrid—where he has been pounding in a half-hearted fashion ever since—made conspicuous gains elsewhere. In fairly rapid succession, Irun, northwestern gateway to France, San Sebastian nearby, Malaga in the south, and then Bilbao, Gijon and Oviedo fell to his arms. The northwestern provinces, with their valuable zinc and iron mines and factories, were completely conquered by late October, and Franco's armies seemed on the march to certain and swift victory.

The government, though it had by now trained and built an army from raw militia, could point to but few military gains. Its outstanding victory was the rout of the Italians at Guadalajara and Brihuega, a defeat prepared and accomplished largely by Russian planes.

Just before Christmas the government launched a surprise offensive against the rather weak Insurgent garrison in Teruel. There was severe fighting in a seesaw battle; the besieged garrison, after bitter resistance in the underground caves and passageways of Teruel, finally surrendered, and at this writing the Insurgents in a counterattack have not succeeded in retaking the city, although their forces have made certain gains outside the town and apparently control part of a dominating hill.

Observers Mystified

Observers here have been somewhat mystified, first, by the government attack, which they held might more profitably have been made elsewhere, and second, by the apparent Insurgent determination to retake the city even at the cost of many casualties and much expenditure of ammunition. They hold that the Teruel salient is too narrow and its terrain too difficult to permit effective launching of a large-scale Insurgent offensive; and they have looked for an offensive elsewhere.

In military strength Franco still apparently holds the odds and the effectiveness of his blockade may come to have an increasing importance. He has about forty war vessels of various types, mostly small, and about 100 armed trawlers, in addition to squadrons of Italian Savoia-Marchetti bombers, all based at Palma, Majorca. He probably has some 400,000 men with some degree of military training, including about 7,000 Germans and 40,000 to 60,000 Italians, 200 to 250 tanks and perhaps 500 planes. He has a considerable artillery superiority over the government forces, and his services of finance and supply are better organized and his civilian population is apparently considerably better fed and less exposed to the abnormal conditions of war than are the troops and the peoples of the government.

Government Forces

The government has some superiority in trained manpower, with about 500,000 men with some degree of military training. This number includes some 19,000 to 24,000 foreigners, including some 5,000 to 10,000 Russians. The government has probably about 200 to 250 tanks and about 375 planes.

In equipment, in leadership, which has certainly not been brilliant on either side; in money, apparently in morale and in the perhaps decisive factor, control of the seas, the Insurgents have the advantage. Despite Teruel the odds are still on Franco, but Teruel proved that the government forces still have a buoyant spirit; they are far from beaten, and the end of the warfare, barring any large-scale outside intervention in behalf of either side, is not in immediate sight.

Behind the Battle Lines in a Devastated Spain

by Alfred Winslow Jones

WE LEFT Spain with overwhelming memories of the war's desolation and not a little relief. From the heated compartment of the Toulouse train we looked out at cattle grazing in the fields and at peaceful, contented villages and thought of what we had seen south of the French border. We remembered the hungry children watching the trucks roll by carrying food to the front, the children in relief headquarters eagerly eating four prunes apiece and calling that a luxury, the 9,000 refugees crowded into a factory building with adequate space for 500—the suffering, the helplessness behind the lines of battle.

We were returning from a tour of inspection with the American Friends Service Committee (Quakers), which is the only nonpartisan relief organization in Spain. The Friends are working in both Loyalist and Nationalist territory, in refugee homes and hospitals for children, in milk canteens and clinics, in emergency-relief war zones, and the Spanish people and authorities have given loyal help and cooperation. As we watched the smoke from comfortable French villages float up into the cold mountain twilight our mixed

From the *New York Times Magazine,* April 3, 1938, copyright © 1938, 1966 by The New York Times Company.

emotions turned into a simple feeling of compassion for those we had left behind.

In the city of Oviedo, in Insurgent Spain, only three houses remain entirely undamaged, yet each day more refugees return to seek shelter in cellars, in habitable rooms of their former homes or with neighbors and relatives. Children are scattered in orphanages for seventy miles around or huddled amid the ruins, sleeping in their dirty, ragged clothes. When forty blankets arrived from the United States it was necessary to distribute them among 652 children. One small boy, for whom there was no blanket left, came up and patted the pile already assigned, then turned away and walked out into the cold of the night.

In a mountain village south of the Biscay coast fifty-four children had been gathered for a meal. They were aged 4 to 12, about half of them boys. They were washed and their ragged clothes were more than reasonably clean, but in most cases their toes protruded from their shoes. They stood for a moment behind their chairs, then sat down and ate slowly and with dignity, although they were starving. Eighteen mothers and twenty older children stood around the room watching. The fathers of most of the children had gone to war on the government side and now were dead or in prison. The children were to return for one meal a day as long as they were hungry and as long as food continued to arrive from abroad.

But for most of these people the problem of clothing was even more pressing than that of food. The textile mills were all in the other part of Spain and many villages in the mountains lie at elevations of 5,000 feet or more, where snow comes early and leaves late.

Some of the bitterest fighting of the war occurred in this country. Homes have been blown up, bedding, clothing, furniture and livestock destroyed as the tide of battle has surged through the villages. There is a refugee population in Insurgent territory estimated at 90,000. The cattle in the upland valleys have been killed for food by the contending armies. Where milk was once plentiful, now there is none. Children with scabies and infectious sores are to be seen everywhere. In one village every family requires help. Even the Mayor's name is on the list of those in dire need.

Throughout areas which have suffered Rebel attacks are spread the effects of the theory of "total war," the purpose of which is not only to destroy the opposing army but also to kill or demoralize civilians. With blockade and food shortage, with aerial bombardment and with the influx of hundreds of thousands of refugees, the strain on the morale is intense.

Through a roadside village between Madrid and Valencia pass long lines of military trucks, heavy with supplies for the trenches. Children watch as the lorries roll by and gather around to talk to the drivers if they stop. The children are pitifully thin and ragged, and they have the brown, withered look that comes with prolonged hunger. Both drivers and children know the trucks are laden with food the children need; but they also realize that the army must be fed first.

In Barcelona, day after day, quiet women in black with market baskets on their arms stand in line at the stores, hoping to buy rice or beans from the limited stock. Alongside the wife of a textile worker may stand the elderly wife of a professor at the university, both with a little money; sometimes food cannot be had at any price.

The air raid brings the essence of the "total war"—the lingering odor of a humble meal, cooked but never eaten, which hangs over a gaping house from the ruins of which rescuers carry a little girl wounded in head and shoulders, and the fragments of a woman; the shambles that once was a doctor's office, where a bomb has ripped away a wall; the cheap photograph, blown from a shattered home into the street, glass and frame broken, and the woman who recognizes the face utters a little cry and picks up the picture.

Victims of air raids are more spectacular than homeless refugees, but there are a hundred thousand refugees for every thousand killed, maimed or left homeless by bombardment. The outsider customarily is shown only the best managed colonies for refugee children, the well-run prisons, the painstaking care bestowed upon art treasures, not the increasingly dirty and hungry people of the warrens where many civilian refugees are housed. This is not because the Spanish people are unaware that foreigners can help, but because their hospitality has a quality of pride which forbids them to embarrass their visitors. Actually the limited amelioration through foreign help merely accentuates the breadth and depth of the surrounding misery.

In Murcia, in the Southeast, is an uncompleted factory building which, had it been designed for human habitation, might have accommodated 500 persons. In it were quartered 9,000 refugees from Malaga shortly after their flight to Almeria. With no soap, no plumbing, no heat and excessive overcrowding, the place was foul; women and children clotted and festered and hungered together until something, although still very little, could be done for them through help from abroad.

Several months after the flood of refugees from Malaga had seeped up through Southern Spain, a new inundation—the victims of the fighting on the Biscay coast—poured into Catalonia. Ahead of them were not only refugees from Malaga but also those who had been evacuated from Madrid, all being supported by a population hard put to support itself.

Many of the children were so weak that only milk and a proper diet could save them. But there was no milk and no proper diet except for the relatively few being cared for in colonies with foreign help. In one such colony the older children learned of conditions among the new refugees and decided to give something of their own food from abroad, "because there are lots of children and they get dreadfully hungry."

Malnutrition is a problem for Spain. Without outside help children in the battle areas will always show the effects of malnutrition and shock, though the work carried on by the American Quakers—los Amigos Cuaqueros, to the Spaniards—indicates the possibilities of rehabilitation. At the time the Quakers began their work the worst of the destitution was in the South, particularly in Murcia. An initial meal of cocoa and bread was provided. Later it was possible to give the smaller children—those under 6—a lunch of four prunes, sometimes with bread.

Children frequently go with their mothers to relief headquarters to get the piece of laundry soap now given to every refugee twice a week. The children often reach for the soap as eagerly as though it were a toy or a sweet. It is easier to understand how the adults value the soap when one sees these people who have lived for two months without it. Dirt, scabies and vermin exist to such an extent that typhus might become epidemic among them if it were to break out.

The hospital in Murcia has only fifty beds; five times as many are needed. There are also hospitals in Alicante and Almeria. Not only sick children are taken in, but also a number of girls from among the refugees who are taught to help with the work and learn the principles of hygiene and practical nursing. Their aid is essential in the Friends' program, for the work is carried on with an administrative staff of no more than ten Americans, who train Spanish helpers to take as large a share of the duties as possible.

Workshops also have been established to help combat the demoralization by providing the refugees with something to do. The girls sew dresses and provide much-needed clothing. The boys make the rope-soled sandals they all wear. Out of the work "clubs" have developed. At first their purpose was to provide the older girls with some escape from the drabness and degradation of their surroundings. Many were being driven into the streets and there was danger of prostitution on a large scale. But when the first story books and games were taken to one of the sewing rooms the girls shouted, "Now we shall be able to study!"

It turned out that at least half of them could not read and many of those who could read "a little" could not write. One wanted to be a dressmaker able to put down the measurements of her clients; another wanted to write to her fiancé at the front. All of them wanted a kind of school. Teachers are hard to find in Spain, but a master was found who would teach the girls in the evenings after his regular work in the elementary schools. More volunteers appeared and the teaching got under way. Initial equipment—books and writing materials—was provided with money raised in England. In many cases Spanish authorities have taken over projects begun with foreign initiative.

Our train rolled into France, and the cattle in the fields lifted their heads to stare. Milch cows. . . . Not long after the Friends opened the hospital in Murcia for refugee children, relief workers found a refugee father and mother and two small boys camped at the roadside near the town. They had foraged for food and found goat's milk for the children. But the milk was contaminated and both boys lay ill with Malta fever, one in a delirium. The mother was afraid to give up to the strangers even the child so desperately ill, but consented when she was invited to spend the night in the hospital with him. There she saw the white sheets, the food, the care of the nurses. It was like another world. The next day she went back and brought in the other child. Both children recovered. And the father brought to the nurses the one offering he could make—two baskets he had woven.

The Nationalists
Enter Barcelona

BARCELONA, JAN. 26.

AMID SCENES OF great enthusiasm Generalissimo Francisco Franco's troops entered Barcelona today.

War-stained units of the Army Corps of Morocco and Navarre, weary but triumphant, were met in the streets by huge crowds which unloosed the pent-up emotion of the last three days. Small columns of troops which infiltrated into the center of the city with the red and gold Nationalist [Insurgent] flag at their head were suddenly engulfed by seething, cheering, clapping throngs.

Your correspondent's car, which was the first to cruise down the great "diagonals" and enter the Plaza Catalunya, was surrounded by crowds of madly excited Barcelonians, who, with red and gold bunting in their hands, mounted the mudguards, footboards and bonnet, cheering with arms upraised in the Franco salute. Tears mingled with the shouting and laughter. The people seemed torn between hysterical abandon and unbelief.

Final Push from Two Sides

The final movement against the city was carried out from two sides, the west and the north. On the west General Juan Yague's Moroccan troops, who had been waiting with ill-concealed impatience on the right bank of the Llobregat River, received their orders at dawn. Three divisions pushed across the river and spread over the country toward the industrial suburb of Sans and the grim fortress-crowned hill of Montjuich, which dominates the harbor area.

A few trial rounds fired at Republican [Loyalist] positions brought no reply. It soon became evident that the Republicans had given up all serious hope of defending the city.

The Nationalist advance was methodical, although uneven. In certain parts long stretches of road were covered without difficulty. In others isolated machine-gun nests would hold up whole battalions for an hour.

But the Republican military machine had broken down. Most of these nuclei of resistance consisted of groups of machine gunners, clinging grimly to their weapons long after the country behind them had been evacuated.

Nationalist infantry, carrying their flags before them, moved ahead, preceded by tanks. Gradually they reduced each center of resistance, thus allowing the main body to push on.

Day Is One of Alarms

The day was one of alarms and excursions. Far and wide around Barcelona the countryside was alive with rumors. From the heights west of the city its brilliant white buildings were visible, glinting in a dazzling sunshine. A huge pall of black smoke rising slowly skyward from behind the Hill of Montjuich, where the Campsa petroleum depot had been burning for two days, accentuated the deathly quietude of the doomed city, waiting anxiously for a decision regarding its fate.

The danger of entering a large city whose will to resist was an unknown quantity was obvious. But both the Moroccans and the Navarrese were straining at the leash. Finally bolder counsel prevailed.

Broken bridges obstructed the progress of the Nationalists, although in many cases destruction was averted by brilliant individual initiative. A bridge at the suburb of Esplugas, for instance, was saved by the heroism of an Asturian legionary who, single-handed and in the face of murderous machine-gun fire, cut the cables attached to a dynamite charge.

In the afternoon the final order was given. Troops waiting in the brilliant sunshine in villages surrounding the city broke into a run and, singing marching songs, made off eastward.

The Navarrese, who had been sent again into the mountains and who had scaled the steep slopes of Tibidabo, a great height overlooking the city from the northwest, pressed down its southern slopes and entered the suburb of Gracia. The Moroccans, who had cautiously taken the hill of Montjuich, over which a white flag had waved from the fortress on the summit since early morning, began to penetrate the gardens surrounding the great buildings built in 1928 for the international exhibition of that year and work over the open country west of the city.

Patrols sent on ahead found deserted streets, which gradually filled with civilians still bewildered. At about 4 o'clock in the afternoon news of the occupation spread around the city like wildfire. A few stray shots from the hill of Montjuich were scarcely heard in the roar of jubilation rising from all sides.

Chaos Found in the City

Chaos reigned in Barcelona. For three days administrative authority had been absent. The only semblance of organization had been that of the Republican Army, laboriously moving tanks and artillery from the city.

The city had been little molested by Nationalist guns and airplanes, although throughout today General Franco's aircraft had been wheeling in reconnaissance flights over the streets.

The harbor district was much damaged, but other areas appeared almost normal. The Republican Army and all Left-Wing sympathizers able to escape had already done so. Coastal roads leading to Gerona and to the French frontier were blocked with troops, material and refugees.

No trace of the Republican Government remained in the city. The few armed men, apart from General Franco's army, were civilian Right-Wing sympathizers who had been maintaining a semblance of order with rifles picked up who knows where.

Large numbers of Barcelonians and refugees were still living in the underground railway, which was filled with chairs, tables, bedding and other household belongings. These persons are breathing freely again.

Most of the important prisoners confined in the seminary of Montjuich and elsewhere had been taken on with the Republican Army into Northern Catalonia. Others were set at liberty.

Barcelona's harbor is at a complete standstill as regards merchandise movement, although merchantmen crowded with refugees had been leaving the port up to the last moment.

Loyalists Blow Up Food Depots

The first time in many months the streets of Barcelona were fully lighted tonight. Troops were bivouacking in the open while billeting officers searched busily for quarters.

It is still too early to estimate how much damage the city has suffered. The people bear obvious traces of prolonged starvation in their faces. They ask a stranger hungrily for food, wine and cigarettes. Considerable stores were removed by the Republicans when they retreated, and others were blown up, notably the great "Bau" deposit near Hospitalet, which contained more than thirty thousand liters of olive oil. One radio station was destroyed.

It is thought at least 800 political prisoners have been removed.

It is estimated more than 200,000 persons left Barcelona with the Republican army, although the population remains swollen greatly above normal.

The bulk of Republican aviation followed the government army.

Hospitals in Barcelona are filled to overflowing with wounded Republican militiamen.

The radio is busily proclaiming the beginning of a new regime. Orders are constantly being transmitted to various departments of the Nationalist military and civil administrations.

The following proclamation was issued:

"Barcelonians, do not fear! The Red rulers who have cheated you will never return."

The first Nationalist newspaper published in Barcelona since the beginning of the Spanish civil war will appear early tomorrow. It will be called the Official Gazette and will continue until normal journalistic activity is resumed.

ENTRY MADE AT 2:30

BARCELONA, JAN. 26

AT 4:30 THIS afternoon the writer entered Barcelona with Generalissimo Francisco Franco's triumphant troops. At the last moment Barcelona's resistance had collapsed completely, and General Franco's army had entered two hours earlier almost without firing a shot.

It appears highly probable that General Franco will move his government here immediately.

A lorry loaded with musical instruments and bandsmen halted in the Plaza Catalunya. When they struck up the Franco hymn, about 5,000 joined in the singing.

From other trucks passing through side streets relief workers were handing out tins of condensed milk, sardines and tunnyfish, white bread, sausage and chocolate bars. [Barcelona advices to The Associated Press said 1,764,000 pounds of bread, 60,000 cans of milk and 200,000 portions of meat were handed out.]

Some packages were flung through open doorways and windows, some crashed through window panes, but nobody cared.

Last night Ruchdu Emiral, the Turkish commercial agent in

Barcelona, went to San Elias Prison, where 600 men were held, and to Las Corts Prison, where there were 600 women prisoners, demanding their release. The prison governor immediately complied. Some of those freed had spent two years in cells. Today General Franco opened the Montjuich Prison, holding nearly 2,000 men, the Model Prison, holding 3,000 men, and the Estado Prison, holding 1,500 men. These freed political prisoners roamed the streets nearly delirious with joy. General Franco's soldiers scoured the streets, looking for relatives among those released.

As dusk fell the streets were filled with milling crowds, some laughing and some singing, but many weeping as they learned of relatives who had fallen in Spain's bitter struggle.

General Franco's troops today captured first the station of the Barcelona subway system at Hospitalet, the first few hundred yards of tramlines and a race track. Your correspondent followed the troops from Hospitalet through Esplugas to the Barcelona suburb of Sarria, waiting there while the soldiers slowly cleaned up, house to house, in the face of desperate resistance.

In the suburb of Esplugas civilians hung from windows and balconies bed sheets or table cloths or anything white as symbols of surrender.

As the Nationalists entered the streets, all shutters stood open, as closed shutters invite a spray of machine-gun bullets, just in case they hide snipers.

Among almond trees in flower and olive groves freshly green in the sunshine, General Franco's troops slowly closed in on Barcelona—nearly 100,000 of them, by this writer's estimate.

Alongside the road columns of troops and transport waited for the word to go forward. Fleets of motor trucks loaded food for hungry Barcelona.

Having taken Tibidabo Hill, Montjuich and Vallvidriera, the Nationalists were ready to drive into Barcelona proper, when it was noted that flags of white and the Nationalist colors were appearing everywhere in the city. Barcelona had given up the fight.

Units of the Nationalist fleet steamed into Barcelona harbor today, dressed overall with the Nationalist colors.

The newly appointed Mayor of Barcelona, Miguel Mateu, head of the Hispano-Suiza motor firm, stationed Civil Guards, shock police and special police throughout the city to prevent looting. They were needed most around the kiosks, where the ravenous citizens were almost uncontrollable.

The news of Barcelona's fall was greeted throughout Nationalist Spain by peals of bells and crowds shouting and singing in the streets.

Part 3

INTERNAL POLITICS

NOTHING ABOUT the Spanish Civil War presented a greater challenge to the ability of journalists than did the reporting of the internal political developments on each side. The Republican government would have liked the outside world to suppose simply that a legitimately elected parliamentary government was defending itself against international fascism and that no far-reaching social revolution was occurring or would occur. The Insurgents wanted the world to believe that they were fighting simply to restore law and order and that all the "healthy elements" of Spanish society were wholeheartedly united behind General Franco. Neither side wished to acknowledge either important foreign influence or the deadly tensions among its own supporters.

Herbert L. Matthews' piece on the leaders of the International Brigades combines empathy in the character sketches with such information about the individuals as they, and the censors, would permit the outside world to receive. William Carney's article, datelined from Paris, conveys the suffering and tension within Madrid. It is the work of a man who is "spilling the beans," knowing that he will not again write from within Loyalist territory. What he says about censorship, surveillance, fratricide, and the physical destruction of the city is fully accurate. He is good on Franco's cautious tactics and military conservatism, and on the general course of the siege, but he is wrong in his apparent assumption that the Insurgents could have walked into Madrid on November 3 or 4. His personal experiences with illiterate militiamen have the ring of truth and also help the reader to place the writer's feelings in perspective. On several points concerning which he had to sift rumors and play his hunches Carney is inaccurate. There were no Russians in the International Brigades except for a few commanding officers, and he greatly exaggerates Russian influence in planning the defense of Madrid, though he is correct about popular gratitude toward the Russians. Twenty-five thousand is undoubtedly an exaggerated figure for the number of "red terror" deaths. The International Red Cross delegates and Basque officials concerned with prison conditions estimated that about six thousand persons were assassinated, most of them in the three months preceding the arrival of the Insurgents at Madrid in the first days of November.

The articles concerning the death of Andrés Nin are also datelined from Paris. The August 8 item is very good in summarizing Nin's career, his relationships to the Republic, to Trotsky, to the POUM, and to the leftist uprising in Barcelona in May 1937. Joaquín Maurín, referred to as having been executed in the Franco zone, was indeed imprisoned but was saved by his family relationship to a bishop, and is today quietly living in New York. The Matthews article concerning dissension within Loyalist ranks is accurate in describing the lineup for and against the Negrín cabinet, the Communist position that Spain was not yet ready for a socialist revolution, the public demands that Nin be produced and prosecuted in open court, and the clearly phony nature of the official version of his "escape." But Matthews seems unnecessarily to accept government propaganda in referring to Largo Caballero as supported only by the anarchists. A large proportion of Socialists and of unaffiliated republican soldiers interpreted the fall of Largo Caballero as a sign of dangerously increasing Communist power within the Popular Front.

The Matthews article on anarchism points up very well both the importance of the anarchists and the problem which they posed for the Negrín government. Matthews recognizes the successful agricultural collectives of Aragon and at the same time notes the strong resistance of prosperous Catalan and Valencian peasants to collectivization—and the support which that resistance enjoyed from the Spanish Communist party. His definitions of libertarian communism and of anarcho-syndicalism provided American readers with clear and valid definitions of political movements having no parallel in contemporary American experience. There are two slight errors worth mentioning: Bakunin's emissary in Spain was named Giuseppi Fanelli (not Farinelli), and Francisco Ferrer was a theoretical anarchist and an anticlerical schoolmaster but no revolutionary leader.

Lawrence Fernsworth's article, datelined Perpignan, reported the efforts of the Catalan regional government to reach an understanding with exiled Catalan businessmen. Fernsworth was close to President Companys of the Generalitat, and sympathetic to the Republican cause without glossing over unpleasant truths. He is generally correct in his assessment of public feeling toward the anarchists by the end of 1937, but the reader should realize that there was considerable popular support for much of the anarchist program during the early months of the war. Harold Callender's article is objective in tone and reveals facts which he had accumulated on his travels but could more freely publish from Gibraltar. Matthews, Fernsworth, and Callender all illustrate how excellent journalists could pursue the facts in difficult circumstances and write objectively about people with whom they had to maintain complex official and personal relations.

The article on the Casado coup highlights the decomposition of the Republican government after the fall of Barcelona. President Azaña had resigned. The continuing authority of the Negrín government was challenged on three counts: its impotence, its absence in France, and its lack of constitutional legitimacy after the president's resignation. The Casado group acted in order to end the war quickly, and with the false hope that they might obtain better terms from the victor.

Sketches of the International Brigades

by Herbert L. Matthews

MADRID.

WARS WITHIN wars are being fought on Spanish soil today. There is a Spanish civil war; there are German and Italian civil wars on a minor scale; there is a sort of European war of Germany and Italy against Russia; there is a class war of the most involved sort that has brought the proletariat against the upper classes, and left wingers and moderates of all sorts against fascism, so that many people have been led to call this a war of ideologies. The armies that face each other across the front lines of Madrid are puny compared to the vast forces that have been unleashed throughout the world by General Franco's uprising. This war is like a vortex in which those countries nearest to Spain have been most profoundly affected, but even on its outer edges it has caught up men, parties and classes in its mad round.

It was inevitable that idealistic youth, older men of sincere convictions, soldiers of fortune and, to a minimum extent, adventurers should have ridden that storm and found themselves in Spain, directing troops or firing rifles and machine guns on which-

From the *New York Times Magazine,* January 3, 1937, copyright © 1937, 1965 by The New York Times Company.

ever side they felt to be in the right. For reasons at whose basis lie profound movements of world politics and thought, most of those men have come to Spain to fight on the side of the Spanish Government against the Insurgents. No objective foreigner here can fail to be astounded at the strength of this unformed, unorganized but truly powerful expression of world opinion. Something has started here which is going to make a deep mark on the world for generations to come. No greater mistake could be made today than to consider this struggle merely as a localized conflict.

However, it is much too soon to lose one's self in speculations whose vistas soon become too vast and nebulous to have much worth. It is better to try to understand what is happening here, and one good way to do so is to consider some of these men, who have come from the four corners of the earth to fight for their ideals. There is no use trying to classify them, for they do not bear classification. Some are Communists, some Socialists, some Republicans, Democrats, Liberals, some are just revolutionaries and all are anti-Fascists. Let us just take them as they come.

There is Emil Kleber, for instance, who is the most important figure of them all. He commands the entire International Column, in which is now included a good portion of Spanish troops as well. General Kleber is a Communist. He and Tim Buck, with whom he worked in Canada, have known what it is to suffer prison for their beliefs.

The story of his life reads like a romance. He was born in Austria (Kleber may or may not have been his real name; identities are not too carefully stressed in revolutionary circles). During the World War he was drafted into the Austrian Army and found himself fighting as an officer against the Russians. He was "captured," and "escaped." The quotation marks are used because he smiled slyly and knowingly when he told me about it. Even then his sympathies were with the Communists.

Instead of rejoining the Austrian forces he made his way to Canada, where he somehow maintained a precarious existence until he joined the Canadian force which made a part of the expeditionary army sent to Siberia. That was one way of getting to Russia. Fighting what seemed to be developing into a Japanese war of conquest suited him no more than it did many a sincere radical, and by a process whose details are somewhat clouded he was soon to be found fighting for those Russian forces which were fashioning what was then called the Far Eastern Republic. That was more in his line, and his help was no mean factor in the Russian success. When the Far Eastern Republic became merged with the Union of Soviet Socialist Republics his work was done, and he left Siberia a soldier of experience and great ability in a peculiar kind of warfare.

Years of obscure struggle in Europe and America followed. Communist circles in New York know him well. During those years he became a naturalized Canadian. The next time the world heard about him he was the "General" in command of a Red Army in China—56,000 men, armed with rifles having just twelve rounds of ammunition apiece. It was in Kiangsi and Marshal Chiang Kai-shek, with 1,200,000 well-armed soldiers, had him virtually surrounded.

If anyone could ever get Kleber to tell the story of what followed it would make one of the most thrilling books that ever was written. It was truly an epic. He took his men on a retreat back to Szechwan in eight months, during which they marched about 3,500 miles in a huge arc, defeating force after force which Chiang threw against them, maintaining order and discipline throughout and ending up safe, coherent and out of the Marshal's reach. The greater part of that force, incidentally, is now fighting against the Japanese-armed expedition in Northern China.

His work done, Kleber returned to Canada, where he and Tim Buck worked together. (Buck, incidentally, was also in Spain during the early days of the war.) A year ago he left Canada for Europe and, when the Spanish civil war started, offered his services to the government. He and his column threw themselves against Franco's forces on the day the siege of Madrid started. It was the psychological moment, for it coincided with an amazing spiritual and moral reversal of the Spanish militia.

Kleber is very modest about it, and refuses to take any credit. He is an exceedingly attractive character—a fine-looking man with a winning personality. Despite his long career, he is only

41—a big fellow, heavily built, and with a heavy face, high cheek-bones, broad nose, thick lips, bushy eyebrows. It is a face that might almost seem brutal if it were not for a boyish and ingenuous smile that keeps breaking out, and a good-fellowship and modesty that are unquestionably genuine. He is idolized by his troops, with whom he has fought in the front-line trenches, shooting a rifle with remarkable accuracy and demonstrating a courage that proved contagious. In the troubled and anxious times that face the world it would surprise no one here if Emil Kleber were to prove an important factor.

It would be hard to place Kleber in any particular category. It is true that he is a Communist, but he is not fighting here for communism; he is fighting because his sympathies are with the Spanish Government and people, and because he hates fascism.

Nothing could be more mistaken than to tie any one tag to the forces fighting on this side. Take Randolfo Pacciardi, for instance. He has the nominal rank of lieutenant colonel (ranks are conventional terms to assure proper discipline at the front; behind the lines all are "comrades"). Pacciardi is an intellectual, but a man of action at the same time. The writer mentioned a moment ago that there is more than one civil war being fought in Spain. There is an Italian one, for example. On this side the Italians are in the Pacciardi Battalion, and their ranks are growing at such a rate that they hope soon to have a "Pacciardi Brigade."

Their leader is a lawyer—handsome, cultured, young (about 45 or less) with a World War record so fine that he was recommended for the highest award in the Italian Army—the Gold Medal. After the war he entered politics, not as a Communist or even as a radical, but as a republican. The word "republican" did not mean that he wanted to make Italy into a republic, but it was used as an expression of liberalism and democracy. He formed a war veterans' organization of men sympathetic with his ideas. In a famous law case that Italo Balbo, now Governor General of Libya, brought against a Socialist newspaper in Ferrara, Pacciardi successfully defended the newspaper.

It goes without saying that such a man became persona non grata when the Fascists took power, and one fine morning he fled to Switzerland an hour or so before the police came for him. As happened with so many of his associates, Switzerland did not welcome him either, and he ended in that haven of political refugees—Paris. There for years he successfully pursued the profession of journalism. He is happily married; he was earning a good living—and he left everything to fight for Spain, because he felt that it was just and right to do so. His battalion has distinguished itself in brillliant fashion, particularly in the fighting that went on around Pozuelo a few weeks ago.

Pacciardi is just as typical of the foreigners fighting in Spain as Kleber. There are other Italians like him here, but space permits only the briefest mention of two of them. Pietro Nenni, one of the two political advisers to the International Column, is another intellectual. He is a Socialist, and once upon a time he and Benito Mussolini were fellow-workers in a common cause and close friends. Now, so to speak, they are fighting each other. Nenni is not a young man, and not strong. Nor is he a soldier. He is a gentle, cultured individual, whose convictions are so deep that he has sacrificed everything to do his part in combating fascism.

Pacciardi's aide, Umberto Galliani, is also well worth mentioning. He was one of the directors of the New York Stampa Libera, an anti-Fascist newspaper. He, too, went through four years of the World War, and he, too, had his deep convictions, which brought him from his safe and lucrative position in New York to the front lines of Madrid, where he has fought bravely and well.

It was inevitable that anti-Nazis, as well as anti-Fascists, should come here to fight their civil war, too. The Germans are mixed in with men from France, Poland, Czechoslovakia and other Continental countries in the Eleventh International Brigade, which, however, is commanded by a German. His name is Hans—just Hans, and nothing more. Nobody knows his last name, and nobody cares. He has relatives in Germany and it would be unhealthy for them if the Nazis learn exactly who Hans is.

He is 38, married, tall and dark—not what would be chosen in Germany now as a Nordic in appearance. Before the World War he was a cadet in a military school, for he comes of a good family.

During the war he was an officer in the German Army, and he fought well. But what he saw then made him hate nationalism, and he became a journalist for radical newspapers. In the struggle against Hitler he was on the losing side and had to leave Germany.

Thus far his case was that of thousands of refugees. However, he was not content to accept his fate passively. During the Asturian revolt here in 1934 Hans came to Spain to help the miners, who were suppressed with a ferocity and cruelty that provided one of the causes for the present division in Spain. So when the civil war started Hans had no hesitation. Leaving his wife and his job in France he came here, as he says, "to defend liberty."

If names are wanted, here is a well-known one: Gustav Regler, the German author. Regler comes of a Catholic family, and as a boy he was educated in a Catholic school. Intelligent and sensitive, he had a long internal struggle during his youth, from which he emerged as a free-thinker. He, too, is 38, with a pale, lined face, and a nervous tick of the mouth that gives him a peculiar aspect of intensity, and even grimness. But he is not a forbidding character at all, and, in fact, is one of the most popular men of the International Column.

The Nazis had no love for him. One of his best known books is about the Saar, "Under Cross-fire," and it painted a picture which would have made the Saar an unpleasant place for him to remain in even if he had not also taken an important part in the political struggle which preceded the plebiscite. He lost his German citizenship, and went to France. When the civil war began he helped to raise the money whereby French workmen gave a group of trucks to the Spanish Government's cause, and he came here with those trucks. Because he spoke French so well, and was not too strong, he was made political commissar of the Twelfth Brigade.

Another German political commissar was Hans Beimler, who was killed in action several weeks ago. He was one of the most important figures in the column, and his loss has been deeply felt. Beimler was a Bavarian, whom the Nazis put in the Dachau concentration camp. In some way he escaped; his widow is still being kept hostage in Germany. He was the real leader of the German Communists here, and although his job was political commissar of the Thaelmann Battalion, he could not resist the chance to take an active part in the fighting. His body is now on its way to Moscow for burial.

Perhaps too much emphasis is being placed on the leaders. The rank and file are well worth considering, too. There is Paul, for instance. Here, again, we will not mention last names. Paul is a "non-commissioned officer"—or rather the equivalent of one— of a machine-gun detachment. He comes from Western Germany, is 27, stocky, blond, quiet. When you ask him about politics he looks blank; there is no such thing so far as he is concerned.

He was a worker in a metal factory until 1934, and because he interested himself too enthusiastically in trade-union activities he was expelled from Germany. Then he went to France. A rather turbulent spirit, he even managed to get put out of that easy-going country on two occasions. The second time he went to Switzerland, and just as they were about to put him out of that country the war started here and he came to Spain, where, to use his own words, "the fate of people like me will be settled."

And now meet Ernest, who is a Frenchman in the same brigade. He seems to be about 30, and just a short time ago was a foreman in a factory in France. The uprising here somehow stirred him deeply, and he volunteered to fight for the Loyalists. The day he was called his father died, but he went the next day, leaving a family and a good job. When I asked him why, he could not quite explain. "I just felt I had to go," he said.

The other day, eating our wretched meal at the Gran Via Hotel, we had an English youth with us—red-cheeked, healthy, blowsy, with a shock of chestnut hair that seemed as if it never had a comb. He was David MacKenzie, son of the Rear Admiral of that name in the English Navy—a Marlborough School boy, something of a black sheep at the moment, only 20 years old. He ran away from home because something called him. Adventure? Idealism? Convictions? All of them, no doubt. Now he is a machine-gunner, and an expert one at that, who has made a fine record in the recent fighting.

He has a friend with him, Esmond Romilly, nephew of Winston Churchill. Romilly is 19 years old, and he was expelled from

Wellington because he started a Communist magazine, which, incidentally, MacKenzie distributed at Marlborough. He, too, is in a machine-gun detachment.

One more German is worth mentioning: Alois Weissgaerber, who, like Regler, comes from the Saar. Weissgaerber is a sort of "lone wolf." When I asked him whether he was Communist, Socialist or what, he answered simply, "I am a Catholic." He was a metal worker who organized a sort of Catholic party against the Nazis in the Saar. After the plebiscite he had to go, of course. He always lived alone—a stolid, silent, morose young man. He, too, felt that his convictions made it necessary that he come to Spain and fight.

He landed at Valencia, and began to make his way to Madrid. He came across a truck lying abandoned alongside the road which had been discarded as useless. Being an expert mechanic he tinkered with it and repaired it until the motor functioned well enough for him to drive here. He got a pot of red paint and made red crosses on the sides and top. Now it is an ambulance, and Weissgaerber is the star ambulance driver of the International Column. His comrades cannot speak too highly of his courage and self-sacrifice in taking back the wounded. Curiously enough (or perhaps it is not so curious, after all), he has become much less morose in recent weeks, and much more human.

The list could be extended indefinitely. Some very important names have not even been mentioned yet. There is André Malraux, the famous French novelist, whose works are well known in translation in the United States. He is that almost unique combination of the creative man of letters and the man of action. One of the Loyal air squadrons bears his name.

There is General Lukacs, commander of the Twelfth Brigade. He is a pacifist, of all things, but somehow has found it necessary again and again to fight for his beliefs. During the World War he was an officer in the Hungarian Hussars (he is a native Hungarian). His district became a part of Czechoslovakia after the war. Feeling that communism held the possibility of bringing world peace, he joined the Soviets and found himself as divisional commander in the Red Army fighting against Kolchak. The Russians having won, he retired, like Candide, to cultivate his garden. Now he is fighting again, and when I asked why, he gave three reasons: because he hates Hitler, and "this is Hitler's war"; because Franco is killing women and children; and because in spite of his communism he has democratic ideals.

A curious mixture, indeed, but there are many such in the International Column. A more understandable case is that of André Marty, the French Communist, after whom a battalion is named. He and Pietro Nenni are political advisers of the column as a whole. Marty is particularly famous for having organized the French naval mutiny in the Black Sea during the Russian civil war in 1919.

A whole article could be written about the doctors who have given up their practices to tend the wounded here.

One conviction animates all the foreigners. Whatever they may or may not be, they all hate fascism.

Uncensored Report on the Siege of Madrid

by William P. Carney

PARIS, DEC. 6.

ALL SEMBLANCE OF democratic forms and usages of government has disappeared in Spain, and the first sensation of a newspaper correspondent on arriving in France after covering the civil war for four and one-half months is one of profound relief from strain —relaxation from fettering restrictions, as though a great burden of prohibitions had been lifted from his shoulders.

There is no freedom whatever allowed journalistic investigation, and the strictest censorship imaginable is imposed on all news dispatches sent out from Madrid. Anyone engaged in reporting the course of events is in danger of being seized as a spy and perhaps shot summarily before he can prove his innocence.

Any account of anything which is not favorable to the government is unacceptable to the censor. There is also the constant danger of being denounced as a Fascist sympathizer by someone who has only a real or fancied personal grudge against you.

Hundreds of luckless Spaniards who held the most liberal political views have been slain in Madrid because they were denounced by former servants who were discharged for incompetence.

The intolerance of the Spaniards embroiled in the fratricidal strife has become so intense that an impartial foreigner cannot be friendly with two Spaniards whose political beliefs are even slightly in conflict. If a Communist or Anarchist saw me conversing with another acquaintance whose political affiliation was less radical, all my movements would be shadowed and I might be under the surveillance of "public investigation brigades" for days.

On one occasion I was followed by a public investigator for hours until finally one of the guards in an American bank assured him I was not an enemy of the régime. All my local telephone conversations were listened to by the Bureau of Public Investigation Service.

Once I was denounced as a spy by a drunken Polish volunteer aviator in a public bar after I had declined to drink with him. I had to go to a near-by police station to establish my identity, but fortunately a French volunteer flier who knew me accompanied me and vouched for me. When I visited a big dam near the source of the Alberche River to see how much water had been released through its sluice gates to flood the territory where the Insurgents were advancing toward Toledo late in September, I was arrested in the village of El Templo by illiterate militiamen, who insisted I was a German and to whom my passport meant nothing because they could not read.

Held for Several Hours

Although I was in a War Ministry automobile and accompanied by two militia guards from Madrid, I was not released until several hours later, after being interviewed by a military commander who, happily, knew how to read.

Nevertheless, the vigilant and still suspicious militiamen who arrested me seemed to think I had hoodwinked their chief. They followed me again, but the War Ministry guards with me won a lively argument with them.

Bombs from enemy planes first shattered all the windows in my apartment early in November and two days later damaged it so much it was uninhabitable and thereafter I had to go to the American Embassy to live. But perhaps the most disagreeable part of my work was being obliged to walk home in pitch darkness late at night from the telephone building, where all the correspondents had to do their censored telephoning.

We had to wait for hours for our turn after booking our calls because there was only one line in service to Paris and London by way of Valencia and Barcelona. All street lights were extinguished at 10 o'clock early in the war, and beginning late in October the curfew hour was moved up to 8 o'clock.

We had safe-conduct passes, which we had to produce every 200 or 300 feet upon being challenged in the darkness by nervous young militiamen who read them under flashlight while keeping one covered with an ugly black automatic pistol, usually of large caliber.

Vast Section Devastated

Almost five weeks after the siege of Madrid by General Francisco Franco's Insurgent army began, one-fourth of the city had been devastated, and it is now believed that perhaps three-fourths will have to be virtually destroyed before the Rebels can take full possession.

There is every indication that General Franco could have entered the capital when the government fled to Valencia. But that opportunity escaped him. The defense was thereafter organized in a more efficient way, and it has become a question of battering ahead against well-armed and well-directed defenders.

On November 7, when Premier Francisco Largo Caballero and his Cabinet departed, the Ministers frankly admitted, it was learned from informed sources, that the government considered the situation hopeless and was prepared for a major event within twenty-four to forty-eight hours. The defending militia was at that time demoralized and disorganized. The civilian population was also demoralized as a result of aerial and artillery bombardment. But for some undisclosed reason—possibly because of his ultra-conservative policy—General Franco did not seize his chance to enter the city then and there. We who were in Madrid could not understand why.

Crisis Ended by Outside Aid

Then the Madrid Government began receiving arms, munitions and men from outside. There came tanks, guns and airplanes from Russia, and other munitions and assistance, it seems probable, indirectly from France. Besides, there were foreign volunteers—the International Column, as they have been termed—comprising the Tenth, Eleventh and Twelfth Battalions. They were mostly Russians, but included Poles, Germans, Austrians, Frenchmen and anti-Fascist Italians, with a small sprinkling of British Communists.

Thus what started in July as purely a civil conflict between Spaniards is gradually spreading into an international war in which elements from all parts of Europe are joining according to the ideas they profess. Men of many nations are fighting in the Loyalist front lines and there are signs that the complete direction of Madrid's defense is shifting into foreign hands. For a long time the defenders have been accepting help from foreign advisers.

Foreigners in Rebel Ranks

On the Rebel side German and Italian aviators are reported fighting for General Franco, whose troops include Moors and men of the Spanish Foreign Legion. But the leadership still remains in the hands of Spaniards, who are perhaps dependent, like the Loyalists, on outside help for men and supplies. How long this enlarging conflict can be prolonged is difficult to estimate.

General Franco has consistently shown himself to be cautious and conservative. It is said of him that he never puts his right foot forward without first consulting his left. It took him a long time to relieve the Insurgent cadets holding out in the Alcazar in Toledo. In fact, all hope of relief there had been nearly despaired of before his forces entered the ancient imperial city of Castile.

The Rebels, it is generally believed, have no more than 30,000 men to take Madrid, which is defended by a militia force estimated to number from 50,000 to 100,000 men.

The Insurgent tactics have always been to prepare thoroughly for the capture of any objective by an intensive artillery and aerial bombardment. General Franco cannot afford to lose many men storming an objective; hence he strafes it thoroughly first with heavy artillery and his trimotored bombers.

Same Tactics Followed Now

So far he has followed these tactics in his siege of Madrid. In the Arguelles quarter and especially around the Model Prison, which is on the fringe of Moncloa Park, the Insurgents have been following this procedure. Government forces already have been slowly pushed back from the prison jail to Vicente Ibáñez Street and then back two more blocks to Guzman el Bueno Street.

Heavy shelling first reduced that region as well as the vicinity of the North Railway Station to a shambles before General Franco sent forward any men. Tanks, preceding infantry well armed with hand grenades, slowly advanced after nightfall into the quarters, which had been mercilessly bombarded all day.

If serious resistance is met, the Insurgents usually fall back and resume their bombardment the next day. Apparently General Franco intends to approach the center of Madrid only from the north and the northwest. His men are already in the Casa de Campo, the vast park just across the narrow and shallow Manzanares River opposite the North Station.

After crossing the Franceses Bridge just below the North Station, their line of march would be along the Paseo de Rosales and then uphill in the direction of the National Palace and the Montana Barracks. They might join forces at the Plaza de España, with comrades advancing from the Model Prison along Princesa Street toward the Montana Barracks, but to do this they will require, if the present tactics are followed, the support of heavy bombardments, which accounts for the prediction that three-fourths of Madrid may yet have to be destroyed.

City Is in a Strong Position

To get a clear conception of what this siege is like, it is necessary first to consider the city itself and its surroundings. Madrid cannot be considered an open city. It is in a strong position and is fortified as well. Every one, including women and excepting only children, has been put on war duty. Above the river, from the side the Rebels seek to advance, it is necessary to scale a high hill from the North Station. On the hill stands the National Palace.

It is the Arguelles district that has suffered the most so far. That section is bounded on the west by the Manzanares and on the northwest and north by University City and by the West and Moncloa Parks. It extends northeastward to the Communist working-class suburb of Tetuan de las Victorias, which adjoins the equally Red district of Cuatro Caminos.

The Cuatro Caminos quarter borders on the Chamartin quarter and what is known as the "diplomatic zone." That zone, on the northern side of the city, includes in its area most of the embassies, legations and consulates. It is reached by the broad Paseo de la Castellana, which has been renamed Avenue of Proletarian Union and which extends almost to Cibeles Square, where the War Ministry, the Bank of Spain and the general post office are situated. A few blocks before reaching Cibeles Square the Paseo de la Castellana becomes the Paseo de Recoletos. The diplomatic zone is bounded on the east by the Salamanca district.

Rebel Offer Spurned

General Franco's offer to respect both the diplomatic and the Salamanca districts, if they were not fortified and if government artillery were not placed in them, was rejected by the Loyalists at the beginning of the siege. Nevertheless, these quarters have not been bombed from the air or shelled, with a few exceptions on the outskirts of the Salamanca district.

Leaflets signed by General Franco and dropped on the city by his air raiders as late as Nov. 21 advised all women, children and sympathetic non-combatants to take refuge in the northeastern part of the city. All other sections of Madrid—especially the center, where nearly all the Ministries are clustered—have been bombed and shelled heavily.

Machine guns and ridiculously ineffectual anti-aircraft guns firing one-pound shells are mounted on the tops of all the ministries and tall buildings in the center of the city, such as the Fine Arts structure in Calle Alcala, Madrid's main street, and the Palace of the Press in the Gran Via, or Broadway.

Batteries of six-inch guns have been placed in Callao Square, directly in front of the Palace of the Press, and in one corner of the Retiro, the vast public park, near the Prado Museum, the observatory and the Ministry of Public Works.

Damage to Buildings Heavy

Many apartment buildings in this vicinity and in the southeastern part of the city have suffered badly from bombing and shelling because of the near-by presence of the Leftist artillery, which was easily located by Rebel scouting planes.

The Atocha or Andalusian Railway Station, where more batteries were placed, and the Hotel Nacional, facing it just across the square and fully occupied by Loyalist militia, also were justifiable targets for the Insurgent artillery and bombers.

Observation posts for the government's artillery are stationed in the towers of the taller buildings in the business center of the city and hence the non-combatant inhabitants of this congested area cannot expect to be spared as long as observers controlling the fire of Loyalist guns by telephone remain on the top floors of the city's skyscrapers.

It is evident that the Rebels know where the government's guns and artillery observers are because direct hits have been scored by shells and bombs on the War Ministry, the Atocha and North Railway Stations and on the Madrid-Paris department store building, which houses the Union Radio station and the Socialist evening newspaper Claridad, the organ of Premier Largo Caballero.

Rebels Disclaim Responsibility

It cannot be helped that women, children and aged persons have taken refuge in the basements of these structures, say the Insurgents, who maintain that the Leftists ruthlessly expose them to danger by housing them in buildings that have been converted into fortresses.

It is argued that the government has made itself responsible for all the harm that may befall civilians by attempting to defend what the Rebels term an unfortified open city.

Leaflets distributed daily by Communist, Anarchist and Syndicalist organizations urge and instruct the populace to continue its resistance—"even to the last breath"—as the enemy's troops penetrate the streets of the city.

"Let every house be a fortress," one leaflet said. "Fire on troops from upper-story windows. Fill a bottle with gasoline, stuff cotton in the mouth, ignite and throw it at the enemy's tanks. Build barricades in every street with anything available. If Madrid is to fall into the enemy's hands, he must find only heaps of ruins and piles of dead."

Of course, it is far from true that all of the unhappy resident population left in Madrid is in complete accord with this ferocious proletarian-directed determination to defend the city unto death.

Many Favor Neither Side

There is a considerable section that wants neither Fascist nor Red rule, but everybody, even including the children who go from house to house and through the streets passing collection boxes for various Leftist relief funds, has been mobilized or at least pressed into what proletarian leaders have conceived as a great militarization scheme.

Middle-class shop clerks, bookkeepers, bank employees and other office workers who were not previously organized have been terrorized into joining either Marxist or Syndicalist labor unions. Once enrolled, they have no choice about fitting into the militarization plan. Some of the luckier ones among those with no taste for front-line fighting have managed to be put to work digging trenches or building barricades, while others have been assigned to employment in the haphazard emergency agencies struggling with the problem of provisioning the militia and the civilian populace.

Meanwhile Madrid is hungry, heatless and homeless to a large extent, and is mostly unwashed. There is scarcely any coal to warm the shivering occupants of the houses, apartments and tenements still standing, which have had most of their windows shattered, allowing the bitter winter winds from the mountains to sweep through them. Most of these unfortunates pass almost sleepless nights huddled in poorly ventilated cellars because they are too terrified to remain above ground after a death-dealing bomb has fallen from the sky or a big shell has struck near them.

Militia Still Well Fed

Apparently the government militia still is being fed adequately, but only a few crumbs are left from their mess table for the civilian populace. Potatoes, eggs and meat are rare delicacies that most civilians have not tasted for many weeks.

Food cards have been issued to householders and heads of families for the last several weeks, but long before the end is reached of the lines formed outside the bakeries, groceries and dairy stations and near the few butcher shops and vegetable and fruit vendors still doing business, many luckless housewives and servant girls are sent away with empty baskets. As the doors are closed in their faces they are told to come back "tomorrow" with food cards.

For two months there has been no gas for cooking in Madrid because coal is lacking to manufacture artificial gas. Although Madrid's two sources of water supply, both outside the city limits, have not yet been cut by the besieging army, bombs and shells that have made deep holes in many streets have also broken a large number of water mains, resulting in several entire districts being completely deprived of water.

It is necessary for the residents of these districts to carry water in vessels of every description back to their homes from public fountains and pumps—often at a considerable distance—in neighboring quarters.

Thousands Live in Subways

Thousands of homeless families evacuated from villages west of Madrid or from the Arguelles quarter of the city are living in the underground railway system, not only in the subway stations but along the tracks.

They camp down there day and night, cooking, eating and sleeping as best they can. Many have not come to the surface since they went underground to live. Naturally all train service had to be suspended, and judging by the foulness of the air when this correspondent visited a section of the line near the Bank of Spain station, no satisfactory means of ventilating the subway has been found.

Furthermore it is the sad fate of these subway dwellers not to be safe from enemy aviation bombs even in their dark and unhealthful abode, because huge projectiles dropped by air raiders already have crashed through the streets onto the subway tracks below in two places in the heart of the city. Because street car tracks have been torn up by bomb and shell explosions, service on several surface lines has also been suspended. Consequently, quite a number of street railway and subway employes who heretofore congratulated themselves on being exempted from military service are more than a little worried at present.

In view of the general undernourishment, the lack of fuel for heating and the restricted water supply, which limits human cleanliness and sanitary conditions in the city (the streets are washed only by rain nowadays), there is a real danger of a serious epidemic in Madrid. Dead dogs, donkeys, mules and even some humans had to be left lying in the streets under the ruins of buildings for days in the heavily bombarded northwestern section of the city.

The destructive power of 400-pound and 500-pound bombs

dropped by the tri-motored Insurgent planes almost defies description. The bombs can be plainly seen with the naked eye as they fall from the machines, flying at a height of 2,000 or 3,000 feet.

So heavy are these messengers of death that the bombing planes tip to one side and wobble a little as they are released. When the bombs strike the earth great thick clouds of yellow, black and red smoke mixed with stones and brick dust rise several hundred feet.

City Lacks Air Defenses

Eight- and ten-story buildings are partly or wholly leveled. The city is singularly helpless and defenseless against attacks from the air because the government's anti-aircraft armament is practically useless. About a dozen machine guns and one-pounders, handled by woefully inexpert militiamen, have not brought down a single enemy plane so far, all the claims in government communiqués notwithstanding.

Loyalist aviators have grounded a few Rebel machines by good machine-gun marksmanship, by colliding or by locking wings accidentally with their adversaries and being forced to bail out in parachutes.

Virtually all the government fliers are foreigners, the few Spaniards who enlisted in the Loyalist air force at the outset of the war have been shot down long ago. Until the recent arrival of Russian war planes, reportedly numbering 200, with an undisclosed number of Russian pilots, most of the government aviators were Frenchmen who had gone to Spain either because of Communist sympathies or because they had been attracted by offers of generous pay (at first, 25,000 francs monthly, but later, 12,000) and the lure of adventure.

There were also some British, Polish, anti-Fascist Italian and anti-Nazi German fliers in the beginning, but most of these have long since been killed or seriously wounded or have departed because they were "fed up" with the war. Of six young British pilots who joined the Loyalists in the early days of the conflict, only one remains today. Two were killed, one was severely wounded and the two others simply decamped.

Judged on their performances, evidently few of the foreign volunteers in the government air force have been high-grade pilots. They seem to have been made up mostly of machine-gunners and mechanics of French military aviation or commercial airlines, of young British college Communists and of various others with little flying experience.

Russia Plays Large Part

For some time Russia has been running the show in Spain in so far as the Madrid government's resistance to General Franco's Insurgent movement is concerned. Weeks before members of Premier Largo Caballero's comprehensive Popular Front government, including the doctrinally non-political anarcho-syndicalists, decided it was safer for their own skins to move to Valencia, Marcel Rosenberg, first Soviet Ambassador to the Spanish republic, was sitting in at all Cabinet council meetings.

In fact, his voice in these councils was generally understood to carry more authority even than that of the Premier, who has been manfully trying to live up to the title of the "Spanish Lenin," accorded to him by the trade union element of the Spanish Socialist party, which has always aligned itself solidly with the Third International.

It was Mr. Rosenberg who hand-picked the Largo Caballero Cabinet, formed on Sept. 4, to succeed the manifestly impotent Giral government selected by President Manuel Azaña himself largely from members of his own Left Republican party. Mr. Rosenberg decided that Julio Alvarez del Vayo, former Ambassador to Mexico and Premier Largo Caballero's right-hand man, should be Foreign Minister.

Named Envoy to Moscow

Mr. Alvarez del Vayo has written books about Soviet Russia, and in 1933, before the fall from power of Leftists led by Mr. Azaña, he was named as the Spanish republic's first Ambassador to the Soviet Union. The victory of the Right at the general election in November, 1933, however, prevented Mr. Alvarez del Vayo from taking the post in Moscow.

Mr. Rosenberg is known to have insisted that Madrid defend itself after Toledo fell to the Insurgents and it became apparent that the capital would be General Franco's next objective. There was some inclination among the Loyalists as the enemy steadily advanced on the capital to urge the transfer of the seat of government to the Mediterranean seaport, but Mr. Rosenberg firmly vetoed this.

He was more instrumental than anyone else in naming General José Asensio Under-Secretary of War under Premier and War Minister Largo Caballero. General Asensio was chosen to act as technical commander-in-chief of the unified government militia forces.

When the necessity to fortify Madrid and prepare its defenses confronted the Largo Caballero government a propaganda campaign, obviously inspired by Moscow's representatives, was launched on a big scale. Russian ships, loaded with food and clothing bought with funds raised by popular subscription in the Soviet Union, began to arrive at Barcelona, Valencia and Alicante.

Posters bearing huge portraits of Joseph Stalin and quoting his statement that it was the obligation of Russian Communists to aid their brothers in Spain, appeared all over the city. Other posters pointed out that early in the Bolshevist Revolution Petrograd was in even greater danger than Madrid but did not fall. Instead it survived to become the Leningrad of today despite the fact that revolutionary Russia at that time did not have the outside help which she is giving revolutionary Spain.

Soviet Films Are Shown

A gigantic portrait of Stalin was set up in the Puerta Del Sol facing the Interior Ministry. Only Russian propaganda films, such as "Kronstadt" were exhibited in Madrid's moving picture theatres. Ambassador Rosenberg, of course, attended the gala first night performances of these pictures and his arrival in a theatre would be the signal for the audience to rise and sing the "Internationale" with fists raised in the Leftist salute.

Mr. Rosenberg attended mass meetings called as demonstrations of the fraternal solidarity existing between Russia and the Spanish Leftists. Seated on the platform with Mr. Alvarez del Vayo he invariably allowed the Foreign Minister of his choice to do the talking. He would merely acknowledge the Foreign Minister's flowery introductions with a few words of greeting in his soft, high-pitched voice. He is a gentle-mannered little man and in Madrid's exclusive Leftist press he is referred to as "Comrade Marcel."

Mr. Rosenberg was conspicuous among those present at the funerals of Commander Ristori and other Loyalist heroes killed in action. He usually stood beside Mr. Alvarez del Vayo or some other Cabinet Minister.

To arouse the fighting spirit of the people of Madrid the Foreign Minister said in October at one of the mass meetings in Mr. Rosenberg's honor that if Madrid fell the Loyalists would have lost the war. This phrase was incorporated in the text of a big poster which bore Mr. Alvarez del Vayo's portrait and was intended to stiffen Madrid's resistance to the Rebel onslaught.

Just about a month later Comrade Marcel, General José Asensio, then the military chief, Mr. Alvarez del Vayo, who also was Chief Commissioner for War, and the rest of the new Largo Caballero Cabinet, including three anarcho-syndicalists, deemed it prudent to have all their mail forwarded to Valencia, according to the official statement issued then. The capture of Madrid by General Franco would be of relatively little strategic value to him and by no means would it end the war, it was stated then.

Although the people of Madrid know little about Russia it has become the fashion for them to do nearly everything in what they hope is the Russian manner. Government militiamen, receiving ten pesetas per day, eagerly purchase with their earnings peaked caps decorated with the Communist star, similar to those worn by soldiers in the Soviet Army. The regulation caps issued by the government to them with their uniforms resemble the overseas headgear worn by United States soldiers in the World War.

When Comrade Marcel first arrived in Madrid, he was installed with his staff in the Hotel Alfonso, but soon afterward was moved to the more luxurious Palace Hotel, which had been taken over by militia and converted supposedly into an "emergency hospital" a few days after the civil war began.

Russian Cars Supplied

A requisitioned automobile of an American make was immediately put at his disposal and when he was last seen in Madrid, the Russian Ambassador was still using this car, although his government meanwhile had supplied to the Madrid government an imposing fleet of heavy trucks manufactured in Russia. The streamlined, 1936 model automobile in which he has been riding was one of the thousands of cars, including many belonging to Americans and other foreigners, seized by the militia at the outset of the war.

Far in advance of Russia's decision to aid the Spanish Government openly—without, however, withdrawing from the non-intervention pact—Russian war materials, including trucks, planes, tanks and munitions, were reported in the Madrid press as being received by the Loyalist forces and Russian instructors were said to be drilling militiamen at Albacete, teaching them military discipline, how to handle tanks and how to use artillery.

Foreign volunteers, said to have been composed of 2,000 Frenchmen and 2,000 Russians, were being organized at the same time. They were giving instruction to Spanish militiamen at Albacete early in October.

In the early days of the war, before General Franco's men were anywhere near Madrid, many girls from working class families enlisted in the militia and donned the same blue denim overalls—called "monkey suits" in Spain—that the men wore. War was just a lark to them in those days, but four and one-half months later it has become a grim class struggle that now demands that they exterminate or be exterminated.

116 • *William P. Carney*

Free Service for Militia

Throughout August and most of September, shops, cafés and most motion picture theatres were open for business as usual. Restaurants and cafés were invaded by laughing, joking girls and youths of the militia. They received generous service of free food and drinks. The government liberally handed out slips of paper entitling café and restaurant owners to collect payment. Nothing was too good for the militia.

The foreign volunteers have now unquestionably strengthened and improved Madrid's defenses under the direction of their commander, the German-French-Canadian, General Emilio Kleber. General Kleber spent his childhood in Toronto and served with Canadian troops in the World War. Later he fought for the White Russians in their campaign against Leon Trotsky's Red Army.

Another foreign commander is the Austrian General Julius Deutsch, former War Minister and organizer of the Socialist militia of Vienna.

Then there are many Russian officers in the Loyalist Air Force. Others are commanding tank companies or artillery units and some even leading infantry columns. I saw several of these Russian officers at the front in University City. They speak no Spanish but give their orders in French to a Spanish officer who interprets to the men. Classes for instruction of some militiamen in the Russian language have been established in Madrid.

After the Cabinet had left for Valencia on November 7, the new defense junta, on a strictly Soviet model but headed by General Miaja, was organized in Madrid. Members of the Cabinet were replaced in their different Ministries by military officials under the title of Commissars. There were then a Commissar for War, a Commissar for Communications and Commissars for other services, who, presumably, kept in touch with the civil Ministers at the government headquarters in Valencia.

This parallels to some extent the system of control established by labor groups over business and industry in Madrid. Labor control commissioners were established in banks and other business offices to supervise all transactions.

This correspondent is able from personal experience to confirm the existence of these controls. For example, take the radio service. When arranging for a broadcast to the United States the writer was obliged to submit his broadcast text to the Commissar for Communications instead of to the regular news censor and also had to obtain approval for the technical arrangements from the Labor Commissioner in the radio service, who was apparently one of the technicians.

All the hotels now operating in Madrid are under the supervision of commissioners who formerly were waiters, elevator operators and other minor employes.

Censorship by Foreigners

Even the regular censorship has been invaded by foreign inspectors. When the Foreign Office took over the censorship service, a Russian frequently censored the dispatches of French, British and American correspondents. Not long ago an Austrian woman—a former Viennese Social Democrat who had fled to Madrid—also took up work in the censorship of news going out of Madrid.

The censorship established in Madrid, both for the Spanish press and for foreign correspondents, was on lines much more in keeping with Soviet ideas in this connection than with the customs of a democratic regime. All telephoned and telegraphed dispatches had to be passed personally by a censor, and objections that the censors raised were constantly of such a nature as to exact strict adherence to government policy and the removal of all critical statements with regard to the situation in Madrid.

For example, in a dispatch describing an air raid a censor objected to a mention of the fact that a Loyalist plane had been brought down in combat. He asserted that if it was necessary to mention planes being brought down, the planes referred to must always be those of the Rebels.

Translations for All Dispatches

Dispatches submitted for censorship had to be accompanied by Spanish translations, and in one instance this correspondent, when he called to obtain his censored text, was informed by the censor that his copy had been destroyed. Upon expressing his resentment in a somewhat vigorous fashion he was taken by the censor before an Assault Guard, before whom he was charged with having insulted the Spanish Republic. On his explanation that his exclamation had been merely intended to convey dismay, the Assault Guard took no action.

A similar case that involved a British correspondent ended less happily, however, for the correspondent was asked by the Assault Guard what his political affiliations were in England. Upon giving a reply that he was a Conservative, the correspondent was taken to jail, where he was obliged to remain seventy-two hours—apparently chiefly because Conservatives in Spain were in bad odor at that moment.

On another occasion, when stopped by militiamen, this correspondent showed his newspaper credentials, but was asked to explain whether he worked in America for a Popular Front newspaper. The most satisfactory answer under such circumstances was always in the affirmative, which made all parties satisfied and caused no trouble to anyone.

Encounters with militiamen were not always, however, so easily got through, and one incident which occurred to this correspondent was suppressed by the censor when he endeavored to cable an account of it to his paper. The censor observed cynically that the dispatch could be reserved for a future date when the correspondent would probably get more pleasure in publishing it after he had left the country.

In any case, the facts are as follows: at 9 o'clock on the morning of October 4, four National Confederation of Labor militiamen, accompanied by a porter who in the United States would be called a building superintendent, rang the front doorbell of an apartment. On the door was pasted a notice in Spanish and signed by the United States Consul, John D. Johnson. It read: "To whom it may concern. In this apartment lives William P. Carney, citizen of the United States of America. Kindly treat his property as that of a foreigner."

Ordered to Open Door

I asked the militiamen what they wanted. They curtly ordered me to open the door. The building superintendent then also advised me to follow instructions. But I replied that unless the militiamen had an order from police headquarters authorizing them to search my home and were accompanied by a police officer, I, as a foreigner, was not obliged to open the door. To this they replied that if I did not, they would shoot through it and break it in.

Thereupon I opened the door. A spokesman for the militiamen asked me for my papers. I again warned him of my rights as a foreigner and asked him if he had any authorization to search my apartment. He raised his rifle close to my face and said, "This is my authority."

I protested that according to official orders issued some time ago no militiamen had the right to enter apartments either of foreigners or Spaniards unless they had an order from the Direction General of Security (general police headquarters) or were accompanied by a police agent. To this the spokesman answered, "We have finished with all that now."

I then allowed them to search my apartment and showed them my American passport. I handed this document to him upside down, and he gravely appeared to be reading it without turning it, and then returned it to me with a sneer: "You are probably Fascist."

I replied that an American was not likely to be a Fascist, whereupon he assured me that he himself on the previous day captured ten American Fascists living in the very same street where my apartment was situated. I was the only American then living on that street.

I warned this militiaman that I intended to advise both my embassy and General Police Headquarters as well as the Foreign

Ministry of the manner in which the search of my house was carried out. He said:

"Protest to anybody you like. I would search your house even if you were a Frenchman or Russian and we are going to search all foreign embassies, too, very soon now."

When they had gone I telephoned to the Director General of Security. Thirty minutes later two police agents came to my house and expressed regret for what had occurred. They assured me I was quite right in maintaining that militiamen had no authority to enter my apartment. I asked them what I should do if I was again visited by militiamen who demanded the right to enter my home by the authority of firearms. They insisted emphatically that I would not be bothered again.

When I recounted this story to Eric Wendelin, Third Secretary of the United States Embassy, who was acting Chargé d'Affaires, he said a protest would be made and he advised me to come to the embassy to live in the meanwhile if I thought my personal safety was in danger. He added that all of the approximately 150 American citizens still living in Madrid were being advised that day that they could return to the embassy to live if they believed they would be safer there.

Many Go to the Embassy

After the aerial bombardments in Madrid became severe many Americans accepted this offer and at one time, not including guards and servants who also were sheltered on the premises, there were as many as sixty-six persons there. However, upward of seventy Americans throughout remained in their own residences. In the embassy Americans living there were provided with food and beds. Some men had to sleep on mattresses on the floor. Only newspaper men were allowed to leave the building. The embassy maintained an auto service to assist Americans in cases of emergency, but gasoline was extremely scarce and only urgent calls could be answered.

The same sort of foresight which prompted the Cabinet in its abrupt departure for Valencia has been exercised in other domains. Early provision was taken to be certain that the gold reserves of the Bank of Spain should not fall into the hands of the besiegers.

Long before Madrid was in danger, airplanes systematically transported gold into the safekeeping of foreign banks although to this day its whereabouts has not been definitely traced. Some say a large amount went to Barcelona and Soviet Russia while others say a considerable sum is deposited in the Bank of France's branch at Toulouse. There have been reports that some of the Spanish gold found a way into Britain.

There is not, however, so much mystery regarding the amount itself, which, according to the last Bank of Spain statement, was 2,000,000,000 pesetas.

Sometime in the neighborhood of Nov. 20 the Financial Commissioner of the Defense Council issued an order that all national banks should transfer the funds and stock held in Madrid to branch offices in Eastern Spain. The banks were ordered to open their safe-deposit boxes and transfer in the same manner all money and stocks found there belonging to clients.

Foreign banks were invited to do likewise. They refused to comply and at least one prepared to close its offices and wind up its affairs if the invitation was renewed.

One Bank Invaded

Without waiting for approval of the order the Finance Commissioner invaded the premises of one bank and started to carry it out. The order since has been published and now has legal force.

A precaution of like character was ordered early with regard to Spain's immense wealth in art. The El Grecos of Toledo were brought to Madrid before the city was stormed. Many art objects were removed from the capital when fear of a siege developed. Many paintings by Velasquez, Titian and Goya took the quarters vacated by the emigrant gold reserves and were transferred to safety in unoccupied vaults in the Bank of Spain.

After the siege began the whole Prado Art Gallery was dismantled and a large number of paintings and treasures shipped to eastern provinces.

Perhaps the most controversial and revolting features of the whole civil war and siege have been the continuous executions of prisoners who have been guilty of no other crime than their affiliation with some political group or social caste, and the systematic campaign against the church and church education, promoted by the present authorities.

The executions began with the first day of the rebellion, following wholesale arrests, carried out first at night and then in daylight. Some personal instances will serve better than statistics of the dead to give an idea of these unbelievable events.

At first priests and nuns were arrested and I saw numerous bodies lying in streets and vacant lots on the outskirts of the city which, by unmistakable signs, I knew to be those of persons connected with religious orders. Frequently I visited the morgue and saw the bodies of those who had been executed.

There were 125 bodies on Sept. 26, 300 on Sept. 28 and for days the average seldom was under 100. I saw 200 bodies the last time I was allowed to enter, on Oct. 5. At that time the morgue officials expressed the opinion that I was exhibiting unhealthy curiosity and pointedly advised me not to return.

It seems a conservative estimate that up to last week 25,000 persons were executed in Madrid.

Naturally, such a wholesale tragedy makes less impression than individual tales, but such are often open to suspicion of exaggeration. But I am able to give some instances beyond denial. At first suspects were rounded up and shot without any preliminary examination, but later the People's Court was established, before which they were placed on trial.

Four men were sentenced by this court and government authorities made much of the fact that they had been reprieved. Reports of the reprieve were published in all Madrid papers and communicated to the foreign press. Two days later these four men were rearrested and shot without trial.

I have personal knowledge, too, of the case of Admiral Javier de Salas, Minister of Marine in the Lerroux government. Admiral de Salas was arrested in his home and taken to the Model Prison with Martinez de Valasco, Melquiades Alvarez and other former Ministers.

When taken from his cell in the middle of the night he was asked by an armed militiaman why he had been arrested. Admiral de Salas answered that he was unable to account for his arrest except that he was a former Marine Minister and had been seized with several other former Ministers.

Without further questioning he was led into the prison courtyard and the militiaman was aiming a revolver at his head when militiamen on the roof fired machine guns at a group of other prisoners in the courtyard. The militiaman with Admiral de Salas fell to the ground, fearing to be a victim of the machine-gun volley, but soon jumped to his feet and fled.

Admiral de Salas, who had also dropped to the ground, lay as dead throughout the night. The next morning he was able to regain his cell. Several weeks afterward he was again called from his cell and this time he suffered the ordeal he had at first escaped at the hands of the careless executioner.

Names Obtained in Raids

The names of many persons arrested were obtained through raids on party headquarters, where membership lists were obtained. Some of these victims were rescued through the intervention of South American embassies in a style recalling the adventures of the Scarlet Pimpernel.

These arrests and executions have not abated. They have continued even during the siege. On the night the government quit Madrid 1,600 male prisoners in the jails were delivered into the hands of the militia entrusted with conveying them out of the capital. The biggest exodus was from the model prison near University City, which later became the scene of actual fighting.

Some were transferred to near-by points, but the fate of those removed far afield has not been determined. The discovery of two large collective graves, coupled with other evidence, strengthens a presumption that the majority were murdered in two batches Nov. 7 and 8.

As to the anti-religious campaign, which has been so vigorously encouraged throughout the civil war, it suffices to say that the strongest impression one feels upon coming out of Spain is the distinction existing outside between Sunday and other days of the week. So far has the anti-religious movement gone that in Madrid Sunday is precisely like any other day.

Remaining Churches Fortresses

All churches that were not burned have been converted into fortresses. Barricades have been built about them and confessional boxes have been placed outside for use by militiamen as sentry boxes.

It was said in excuse for the burning of churches that the Fascists had been using them as fortresses, but subsequent history shows the value of this excuse. There have been no masses since July, and there are probably not half a dozen priests in the city.

Here again a small personal incident tells more vividly than all these facts the extent to which attacks on religion have been carried. This correspondent, in speaking to a small child of the working classes, used what used to be a common form of taking leave in Spain, the word "adios."

The 3-year-old child rebuked this by saying, "We are at war— we don't say 'adios' any more; we say 'salute,' " and he raised his little fist clenched in the Communist manner.

Officially the government spokesmen deny any anti-religious policy. Premier Largo Caballero's newspaper Claridad says: "We consider it premature to put forth the religious question because nobody has prohibited freedom of worship." Nevertheless, the churches remain closed.

Anti-Stalin Chief Is
Slain in Madrid

PARIS, AUG. 7 [1937].

UNCENSORED NEWS reaching Paris today from Spain throws an entirely new light on the mysterious disappearance and supposed escape from his Madrid prison of the anti-Stalin radical leader, Andres Nin.

Señor Nin, leader of the P. O. U. M. [United Marxist Workers party], a preacher of revolutionary terrorism and once a supporter of Leon Trotsky, became a victim of the terrorism he preached. Nearly a month ago a band of armed men kidnapped him from a Madrid prison, where he had been taken from Barcelona. Although every effort has been made to hush up the affair, it is now a matter of common knowledge that he was found dead on the outskirts of Madrid, a victim of assassins.

Moscow Foe "Liquidated"

By this act there stands "liquidated" the arch-enemy of the Moscow brand of communism in Spain. With his death it would also appear that the P. O. U. M. organization has been broken up. This organization declared Moscow communism to be merely reformism, not the true revolution. In union with anti-Stalinist parties in other parts of the world, it set about to create a Fifth International, having as its ultimate object the overthrow of the Moscow Third International.

Other outstanding leaders of the P. O. U. M. are in prison, facing charges of high treason and espionage. The party has been declared illegal, its headquarters closed and its newspapers suppressed.

Among the ten leaders named in a note of the Ministry of Justice as due to be tried for espionage is Julio Gomez Ortiz, commonly known as "Gorkin," who with Señor Nin was the brains of the anti-Stalin movement in Spain. Although it was previously reported that Gorkin likewise had been kidnapped and assassinated, this report now appears erroneous.

Another of the ten is a former New York newspaper man of Spanish nationality, José Escuder Poverell, now in San Antonio prison in Madrid. Señor Escuder was the editor of P. O. U. M.'s leading newspaper in Barcelona, La Batalla, published in the expropriated plant of a former Carlist newspaper. His contention was that he was merely a technical employe having no part in subversive activities.

About two years ago Señor Escuder was the editor of Ultima Hora, the evening newspaper organ of the Catalan President, Luis Companys. He returned to New York, but after the outbreak of the Spanish civil war again went to Barcelona, where he acted as correspondent for American newspapers.

Of four Americans arrested in connection with a round-up of P. O. U. M. members in Barcelona July 19, three are known to have been freed. The fourth is believed to have been released yesterday.

Charles Orr and his wife, who were doing secretarial work in the P. O. U. M. offices, recently left Spain after a term of preventive arrest. Hugo Oehler was released last Saturday. Wolf Kupinsky, representative of the Revolutionary Workers League in New York, was scheduled to have been released yesterday, although no confirmation has been received.

It is understood that rigid police investigation absolved the Americans of suspicion of treasonable activities.

Señor Nin was Minister of Justice in the Catalan revolutionary government formed last September, but he was ousted in December at the instance of the Catalan Socialist-Communist party. A Catalan by birth, an author and translator of numerous works on communism, he was considered the most intellectual of Spain's revolutionary leaders. He received his schooling as a Communist under the personal direction of Mr. Trotsky, during whose Russian dictatorship days he acted as his secretary. He was expelled from Russia at the same time as Mr. Trotsky. From that time forward he devoted himself to spreading Mr. Trotsky's doctrines in Spain, where he founded a Trotsky or "Left Communist" party.

In the first years of the Spanish Republic, he caused considerable annoyance to the régime and once was arrested by one of Manuel Azaña's Governments and kept in prison several months at Cadiz. On his release he immediately set about forming a workers' alliance, composed of all revolutionary parties except the Anarcho-Syndicalists. This alliance took the responsibility for the 1934 workers' revolution in Catalonia and Asturias. Under the Right Government's repression that followed, the alliance was broken up.

Señor Nin, however, leaped to the fore immediately upon the military rebellion last year, having meanwhile formed a new party. The P. O. U. M. was an amalgamation of his own party and the workers and peasants bloc, another revolutionary party, which under the leadership of Joaquin Maurin had cut a considerable swath in Catalonia.

Señor Maurin was in the Galicia region of Spain when last year's rebellion broke out. Although he managed to establish communication with Barcelona headquarters, he was finally captured and put to death by the Insurgents, who controlled the Galicia region.

Party Broke With Trotsky

Although the new party continued to be called the Trotsky party, it officially denied the imputation, although admitting sympathy for Mr. Trotsky as a well-intentioned leader. It considered, however, that Mr. Trotsky had remained stationary in his ideas and that his Fourth International was a mere paper affair, while the embryonic Fifth International was to be a real vital force to carry the workers' revolution forward. As a result of this discrepancy it is known that P. O. U. M. leaders and Mr. Trotsky were not on the best of terms.

The P. O. U. M. openly took the responsibility for the Barcelona street warfare last May 3 and the sanguinary days that followed. Previously it had been under bitter attack by the Spanish Communist party, and after the May affair the Communist attack was renewed with particular bitterness. In mid-June Señor Nin and numerous fellow-workers were arrested in Barcelona, Valencia and Madrid. One of them, José Rovira, leader of the P. O. U. M. militia column, was recalled from the Huesca front by a military superior and handed over to the police. There were 200 arrests in a single day. Barcelona leaders were conveyed to Madrid, where it was stated they would be tried for espionage.

Efforts to liquidate the P. O. U. M. after the manner of the liquidation of Trotskyists in Moscow did not meet favor with the Valencia Government. The Government apparently was determined that the prosecution of the P. O. U. M. leaders must be along fair lines, and the Nin tragedy undoubtedly is giving the Government serious concern. As soon as Señor Nin's disappearance was announced, the Secretary of the Interior flew to Madrid in an effort to save him if possible. It was apparently too late.

A version of Señor Nin's disappearance circulated at that time was that he was kidnapped by Fascist officers who were trying to take him to the Rebel lines. This version now appears to have been a blind to hide the true situation. Persistent reports state that the bodies of several others were found with that of Señor Nin.

Revolt Threatens Spain's Loyalists

by Herbert L. Matthews

PARIS, AUG. 9.

A SERIOUS POLITICAL crisis is developing in Spain between the Negrin Government, supported by the Communists, and the Anarchists, led by former Premier Francisco Largo Caballero. The Government is striving hard to avert an open rift, but every indication points to an inevitable showdown that will probably provide difficult weeks for Loyalist Spain.

All military efforts are being subordinated to this problem. It seems most unlikely that the Government will attempt any important military action until this political question is cleared up.

Trouble has been brewing behind the scenes ever since the political crisis last May, when Señor Largo Caballero and his Anarchist supporters were ousted from the Government and the more moderate Negrin Cabinet was installed with Communist support. That crisis was the result of a serious state of disorganization and defeatism, coupled with revolutionary efforts of extremists under Señor Largo Caballero, who were subordinating winning the war to carrying out a social revolution within the civil war.

All the moderate Republicans, Democrats and Socialists, aided by the Communists, whose program now is ultramoderate, joined to create a new Government that would concentrate on winning the war and letting the proletarian revolution fade into the background for the time being. For three months that has been their policy.

The army has been reorganized and has showed its new power in the recent sierra offensive west of Madrid. Industry, particularly in Catalonia, has been taken in hand and has been made to yield something like effective results. Public order has been placed largely in the hands of the new carabinieri corps, which has a firm grip on policing in larger cities and most towns and villages.

Meanwhile Señor Largo Caballero, who is bitterly disappointed and angry, has been plotting his return, aided by his personal friends and with the support of a majority of Anarchists and the entire P. O. U. M., the extreme Communist faction. The Anarchists have been ousted, not only by the Valencia Government, but also by the Catalan Generalidad, which had been their stronghold. They have managed to smuggle some arms through, but the government meanwhile had taken away most of what they had. Arrests of Anarchists and P. O. U. M. members have been wholesale.

However, it must be remembered the Anarchists have something like two million membership in Loyalist Spain and they cannot be waved summarily aside. Among them and in the Left wing of the U. G. T. [General Union of Workers] are many thousands of sincere Radicals who feel that Premier Juan Negrin's Cabinet is nothing less than bourgeois. They say in effect:

"We have not gone through all this agony of civil war just to put the same bourgeois clique back in power. We are fighting and dying for the proletarian revolution."

That element will be on Señor Largo Caballero's side when trouble starts, along with more violent revolutionaries and disguised Fascists who have managed to enter the C. N. T. [National Confederation of Workers], the F. A. I. [Iberian Anarchist Federation] and the P. O. U. M. in surprisingly large numbers.

The Government, however, figures to have all the trump cards in its hands.

There are many who would even welcome a showdown now, feeling that this is the time to crush an element which, in their opinion, would lose the war in short order just to bring about a swift social revolution.

The Communists, being good Marxists as well as disciplinarians, take the stand that everything must be subordinated to winning the war and that Spain, in its present stage of social development, is not ready for a proletarian revolution. Moreover, they point to the fact that, unless and until the Government wins the war, there can be no question of a revolution. Consequently they are heart and soul with the Socialists, like Indalecio Prieto and Señor Negrin, as well as the Republicans, Basque Catholics and Catalan Leftists —all more moderate elements—in an effort to unite Loyalist Spain with a slogan of anti-Fascism rather than a proletarian revolution.

That is the background for the present situation, which has been brought to a crisis within the past week by the disappearance of Andres Nin, the P. O. U. M. leader, and the announcement by Señor Largo Caballero that he is going to stump the country in defense of his record and in opposition to the Negrin government.

Señor Nin was arrested in Barcelona last June, when the authorities took the opportunity of the discovery of a Fascist plot in which some P. O. U. M. members were involved to raid the P. O. U. M. headquarters. It was given out that he was taken first to Valencia and then to Madrid for imprisonment pending trial, but somehow no one ever saw him in Madrid or got the record of his arrival. P. O. U. M. members and Anarchists grew more and more insistent in their demands that Señor Nin be produced and tried, until the authorities, unable to dodge the issue any longer, gave out a communiqué last week stating that he had escaped along with his guards.

Outwardly that had to be swallowed. The censors forced even C. N. T. newspapers to print that version. Actually it is firmly believed in P. O. U. M. and Anarchist circles that Señor Nin was murdered en route to Madrid.

[A special dispatch to THE NEW YORK TIMES from Paris last Sunday based on authoritative information stated that the bodies of Señor Nin and several others had been found in the outskirts of

Madrid after they had been kidnapped from a jail in the Spanish capital.]

Apparently the next political development will be Señor Largo Caballero's stump campaign, and much depends on the reaction to it. Señor Largo Caballero has been thoroughly discredited among the majority of Loyalists, but he still has a strong following in labor unions, as well as among the Anarchists, who see in him their only chance of getting back their former power. It may well develop into an open fight on the lines of last May's uprising in Catalonia, and the Negrin government is quite prepared to fight it out. They have the army and the police in their hands, and they believe the vast majority in Loyalist Spain will back them.

Moreover, it is a problem that has to be faced and fought out sooner or later, and as far as the Government is concerned, it is felt that the sooner the better. Nevertheless it is going to be a critical time.

Anarchism:
Spain's Enigma

by Herbert L. Matthews

BARCELONA.

SPAIN IS A symbol and a battlefield for a war of classes and ideologies. Democracy, republicanism, socialism, communism, anarchism —these are the movements whose fates are at stake here on the peninsula in greater or lesser degrees. But Spain is the country par excellence of anarchism and this war, which is changing the face of the earth in so many more ways than people realize, is, among other things, a turning point in the history and development of that movement.

A majority of Loyalist Spain has turned on the Anarchists and is seeking to dominate them and nullify their force in the conduct of government and the prosecution of the war. The Negrin Government is the negation of what the Anarchists are seeking. It is democratic, moderate, even bourgeois, in its policy, although the controlling force, or at least the strongest single force behind it, is communism. Spanish communism is bourgeois at the moment, paradoxical as that may seem. But that is another story; the important thing is that the Communists here are waging a powerful campaign of propaganda against the Anarchists, and the Anarchists, after lying low for a few months, are now showing signs of fighting back. The political development of republican Spain can almost be explained in terms of this conflict: even the outcome of the civil war may depend on its results.

It has been said that every Spaniard is an aristocrat. Certainly he is a being apart from his fellow-beings. He is egocentric, not social, practical, not idealistic. His response is to something which has a direct, personal appeal, such as anarchism, rather than to a call for submergence of his individualism in the state as the Fascist demands, or to an authoritarian society such as communism. There is a deep religious substratum to his character. It compels him to project his personality like a sharp silhouette against "the white radiance of his eternity."

He is not at home in any of what Salvador de Madariaga calls "the middle stretches in which social and political communities lie." Anarchism catches him at the individual end of those two poles, ego and universe, and his response to its appeal is instinctive. Of course, when the time comes to give reality to anarchism's objectives he is only too likely to find out that, despite everything, society impinges on his individuality and he cannot live in a vacuum. Nevertheless, the philosophical appeal is deep and haunting.

To be an Anarchist you must believe that men are essentially good. Hence, it is government, political leaders and institutions which must be bad. Get rid of them and let man be natural and free, the Anarchist philosophy urges. It is a noble ideal, with a mystic and spiritual content that is more suitable to the Spanish temperament than communism seems to be. This is particularly true in respect of the Catalan, the Valencian and the Andalusian.

The philosophical appeal of anarchism to the average Spaniard is through that strong individualism, which is at the base of his character. The Spaniard does not naturally merge into a society or a state. His instinct is to absorb, not to be absorbed. You cannot make an automaton of a Spaniard. For that reason neither Moscow's authoritarian communism nor the dictatorial fascism of Rome and Berlin suits his character. Whatever happens in Spain, neither of those things will have any chance of lasting here.

The numerical strength of anarchism in Spain varies according to who is doing the claiming. The Anarchists themselves say they have 2,000,000 members, while their opponents are unwilling to credit them with much more than half so many.

In the early days of the rebellion a number of Anarchist experiments were started in the provinces of Aragon, Catalonia and Granada. Most of them were short-lived, for the majority of the peasants opposed efforts to anarchize their communities and some sanguinary struggles resulted. In certain towns the experiments proceeded and are only now being liquidated by the Negrin Government, which is determined to maintain general control under war conditions.

One of the more successful efforts occurred at Bujaraloz in Aragon. There 14,000 peasants collectivized 11,000 hectares of land, of which 9,000 hectares were wheat-growing and 2,000 were in pasture. Last Autumn they had a crop of 2,150,000 kilos of wheat valued at 7,000 pesetas. Money was abolished and the surplus wheat was used instead, after deduction of enough for local needs and valorization at current market prices.

That was the basis of the group's barter, and each member of the community had an equal share. Tickets were given out representing the values, and to each person was allotted a certain number for food, clothes, education, hygiene, and so on, while what was called a "prudential reserve" was set aside for emergencies. Every family received ration cards and food was distributed co-operatively. The aged, invalids, widows and orphans were reported well cared for.

On the whole, the experiment seemed to work well for a while, but friction of all sorts apparently was developing. Federico Urales —one of Spain's veteran Anarchists, who is much respected in Anarchist circles—recently issued a blast against all such communities. He asserted that not a single one of the agricultural or factory communities had proved a success; only the transport services in Catalonia had done well.

Anarchism, like communism, derives from socialism in so far

as it advocates the community of property and is identified with the class struggle. However, it is libertarian, not authoritarian. It seeks the realization of its ideals not in Marx's democratic state or Lenin's dictatorial one but in the free and voluntary organization of communes and workers' federations. According to the classic formula of communism, "each one gives according to his capacities and receives according to his needs"; but according to anarchism "each one gives and takes what he wants, and that presupposes abundance and love."

Anarchism in Spain began to gain ground in 1868 (the year of the liberal revolution which ousted Isabel II), when the first emissary of the International, a follower of Mikhail Bakunin, named Farinelli, appeared on the Spanish scene. He found fertile ground for anarchism. The year before that Bakunin had drawn up a loose program for the International Alliance of Socialist Democracy. "The alliance," he said, among other things, "desires the definite and absolute abolition of classes. . . . It desires that the land, the instruments of labor and all capital be the collective property of all society, to be utilized only by workers. . . . It holds that all presently existing States, political and authoritarian . . . must disappear in the universal union of free associations."

Bakunin's final open break with Karl Marx a few years later had its repercussion in Spain at the Congress of Saragossa in 1870, where occurred the profound split which still divides the country. The split centered around Barcelona, which opted for the individualistic, direct action of anarchism, and Madrid, which chose the democratic, political action of socialism. To this day Madrid is the center of socialism and communism, while Barcelona is the fountain of anarchism; but the disciples of the latter philosophy have always been in a minority and have always been persecuted.

Oppression of anarchism and the reaction to it have caused the movement to be firmly identified in all minds with violence. Anarchism in popular opinion is synonymous with strikes, bombings and assassinations, and there is good reason in Spanish history to make that identification. However, theoretically anarchism abhors violence.

There are no really important Spanish exponents of the anarchist philosophy, for the movement here has always been in a process of ferment in which the leaders were actively struggling, rather than formulating theories. Among the few worth mentioning are Juan Serrano y Oteiza, his son-in-law, Ricardo Mella, José Llunas Pujols and, above all, Anselmo Lorenzo, who died in 1914.

The theorist who seems to have made the greatest impression on Spaniards was the Italian Errico Malatesta, whose long and turbulent life permitted him to be in the movement from Marx's days until after the formation of the Second Spanish Republic in 1931.

Malatesta, like all Anarchists nowadays, was a "voluntarist." The program was to be achieved by direct action and was realizable only in proportion as men desired it. Here is a synopsis of that program as Malatesta formulated it at the time of the Second Congress of the Italian Anarchist Union in Bologna in 1920. It contains the essence of what anarchism is striving for:

Abolition of the private ownership of land, raw materials and the instruments of labor.

Abolition of government and all power which the law assumes and imposes on others; therefore, abolition of monarchies, republics, parliaments, armies, police, magistrates and all institutions endowed with coercive powers.

Organization of social life by means of free associations and federations of producers and consumers.

Guaranteed livelihood for all.

War against religion.

War against patriotic rivalries and prejudices. Abolition of frontiers. Fraternity among all peoples.

Reconstruction of the family in that form which results from the practice of love, freed of all legal bonds, of all economic or physical oppression and of all religious prejudice.

There you have the final goal of anarchism, which modern theorists call "libertarian communism." However, like all social ideals, it is not capable of achievement all at once. You need preparatory stages and, in the case of anarchism particularly, you need some practical organizational expression to act as a channel and weapon in the struggle toward the goal. That is where syndicalism comes in.

Spanish workers took so naturally to the syndicalism of Georges Sorel, brought over from France in the latter half of the nineteenth century, that virtually all of them in time became members of syndicates—as they still are today. To the Anarchists it gave immediate fulfillment to their need for organization and collectivization, so that the movement here is always more properly identified by calling it anarcho-syndicalism.

According to Sorel, the producers by industrial not political methods were to organize the economic world. Direct action was to take the form of an industrial war in which the workers of the same industry in syndicates were to be the soldiers who should fight a class struggle with the weapons of the strike, boycott, sabotage, union label and the like. It was syndicalism also which brought the conception that property should be appropriated for the workers. Hence you get your violence, although Malatesta always protested against the identification of anarchism with violence.

The period of particular Anarchist violence was during the minority of Alfonso XIII, when there were bombings, assassinations, incendiarism, strikes, terrorism of all sorts and even revolutionary movements. It came to a particularly severe climax in the Barcelona riots and fires of 1909, after which Francisco Ferrer was arrested and executed along with other revolutionary leaders.

It was two years later that the now all-powerful C. N. T. (National Confederation of Workers) was first formed. It was promptly suppressed, but revived in 1915 and by the time of the Second Republic had a million members. Now it claims something like 2,000,000, of which 1,200,000 are in Catalonia. The C. N. T. is the Spanish organization of anarcho-syndicalism.

Held firmly in check under the dictatorship of Primo de Rivera, it burst out into violent opposition against the republic and for the next five years, until the civil war started, it fostered many strikes and even revolutionary movements.

The more violent and determined members had formed a militant organization at Valencia in 1927 called the F. A. I. (Iberian

Federation of Anarchists), which joined forces with the C. N. T. early in the republic and from then on dominated its councils.

The role of both organizations in the civil war has been unfortunate. The Anarchists have been accused, with only partial justification, of placing the social revolution before the rebellion— of trying to achieve their particular program instead of joining with Republicans, Socialists and Communists in prosecuting the war. In some places in Catalonia and Valencia Province they tried to impose independent communes and collectivization against the will of the townsfolk and peasants. Violence and loss of life resulted in towns like Puigcerda, Bellver and Fatarella.

Meanwhile, the Communist-Socialist U. G. T. (General Labor Union) was cannily backing the peasants. Spain has a predominantly agricultural population which the old governing classes and large landowners were unable to save from misery. The farmer in many sections such as Catalonia and Andalusia was more often than not a desperate, starved, ignorant man, with nothing to lose and an easy prey to propaganda for violence.

At the beginning of the republic, and again when the civil war started, farmers seized the latifundia (wide areas under single ownership) and divided them into strips, thus, with true Spanish individualism, showing a preference for private ownership. The Communists are supporting them against the Anarchists' effort to collectivize the farms, and in that struggle lies one of the fundamental reasons for the present antagonism of the two organizations.

What are the Anarchists going to do now? Loyalist Spain's chances of winning the war depend partly on the answer. They are still a very powerful element—far too powerful to be suppressed. They have pledged themselves to help win the war under all circumstances. But they are apparently determined not to fight a war that will end without a social revolution. Will their ideas on how to win coincide with the Government's?

Catalans Wooing Industrial Exiles

by Lawrence A. Fernsworth

PERPIGNAN, FRANCE (on the Spanish Frontier), JAN. 1.

AFTER HIS RECENT visit to Brussels, President Luis Companys has returned to Catalonia and resumed his position as head of the Catalan Government.

The real purpose of the visit may now be told. It was not, as reported, to begin peace negotiations with representatives of General Francisco Franco—Señor Companys is scarcely the man for that.

It was to enter conversations with "economic elements," meaning business men and financiers, mostly of Rightist tendencies, who had departed from Catalonia in the early part of the civil war and whose property was then seized and collectivized.

The attempt to regain their sympathies may be described as a process of weakening General Franco's support by boring from within.

The Catalan Government, supported by the moderately inclined Central Government, now installed in Barcelona, would like to have an understanding with these men for the restoration of their properties at the right moment and the salvaging of Catalonia's economic interests, of which the chief are her now moribund textile industries.

Exchange Problem Baffling

Catalonia's high finance dreams of underwriting these collectivized industries have not come true. The problem of obtaining foreign exchange is now almost insuperable. It is felt that with the right kind of man in charge and a consequent restoration of confidence abroad, this situation would improve.

The collectivization regime has been disastrous, detested by the great majority of the workers, who find themselves earning less than formerly and their businesses going to pot.

Collectivization has meant either that "what is everybody's business is nobody's business" or that undesirable persons have gained control of the workers' councils for their own private ends. The workers, moreover, are tired of spending most of their free time at workers' meetings.

In a large number, perhaps a majority, of cases the workers were coerced by extremists into voting for the collectivization of their particular industries or businesses.

The interested extremists, principally Anarchists, used arguments of violence and of withholding raw materials that they controlled to accomplish their ends. Now that the Anarchists are being made to toe the mark by the government, the workers feel more assured.

Anarchist Charges Borne Out

The tendency of the Catalan Government toward mitigating if not completely abolishing collectivization bears out the charges made against it by Anarchists and other extremists preceding the street fighting of last May that this government would really like to see a return to a bourgeois regime.

The truth is that Catalonia, despite its large labor population, is essentially bourgeois. So deeply are the roots of "capitalistic proprietors," large and small, sunk in its soil that to uproot them would be to uproot Catalonia itself.

Notwithstanding its revolutionary front and its previous enforced alliance with the Anarchists, the Catalan Government has maintained good relations with many leaders of the Catalan Right party, called the Lliga Catalana, of which Francisco Cambo was the head and which in the elections of February, 1936, allied itself with José Maria Gil Robles' Catholic party.

In the first months of the civil war members of the Catalan Government endangered their lives by facilitating the departure from Spain of many Catalans of the Right who are now living in France and elsewhere.

The writer can testify to this, for he himself was several times traveling aboard British and French warships on which were Catalan political leaders and capitalists put aboard by officers of the government, who in many cases had run the gantlet of Red sentries.

As an instance, in the early days of August, 1936, I proceeded from Barcelona to Port Vendres on the French destroyer Fortune, on which were the former President of the Rightist Catalan Government installed by the Rightist Gil Robles government in 1935 and Manuel Portela Valladares, Spanish Premier at the time of the 1936 elections.

Some of these Rightists, I now learn, have already returned to Barcelona and are walking the streets in perfect security. Señor Portela Valladares is among those who have returned.

In the meantime, the republican government is pursuing its policy of establishing a responsible government from which extremism shall be eliminated. To the Communist party has been given its "proper" niche in the Popular Front government. The Anarchists, having never been members of the Popular Front, have no niche there whatever.

It is General Vicente Rojo, hand-picked by the new government, and not General José Miaja of Madrid—known as the hand-picked man of the Communists—who is chief of the united republican armies.

Although the aim of the government may now be considered

as being the preservation of the republic, it is recognized that certain "advanced" legislation of a social order may have to be conceded in the future because of the important aid that the opposition to the Franco rebellion has received from the extreme Left and the armed masses.

The swing, however, is toward an advanced bourgeois regime. This would mean the undoing of much of the collectivization and even confiscation of property imposed in the early days of the conflict.

The role played by President Manuel Azaña in the policy of regeneration after the bloody convulsions of the first months of the military rebellion is underestimated. He has been widely pictured as a figurehead, a nonentity and a virtual prisoner of the "Reds."

Nothing could be farther from the truth. He has been very much in power behind the scenes in shaping government policy, working constantly with such personages as Premier Juan Negrin and Defense Minister Indalecio Prieto.

Fascist Influence in Spain Growing

by Harold Callender

GIBRALTAR, MAY 16.

IN A SARAGOSSA hotel one night a Spanish officer announced the capture of the town of Caspe. A German, evincing little interest, remarked: "Ah! But we have just taken Vienna."

The Spaniard might have retorted that the German conquest of Austria was the result of the Spanish war or at least that the apprehension caused in Western Europe by the Spanish conflict helped to give Germany the opportunity of unopposed expansion in the east. Whether or not it is the preliminary bout to a greater struggle, the Spanish war has contributed to a shift in the balance of power in Europe and has strengthened the military position of Germany and Italy.

The presence of a large German air fleet south of the Pyrenees and within a few minutes' flight of cities in Southern France will disturb many in France and Britain as long as the war in Spain lasts. Large air fields with concrete runways and underground hangars have been built also. In effect Germany has air bases on both sides of France and both Germany and Italy have strategic positions in Spain which will be invaluable in the event of a greater war.

Footholds Were Price of Aid

General Francisco Franco's assurance that he would not give away any territory seems to French and British critics to be beside the point, since it is not territory but strategic footholds that are in question. Germany and Italy may not keep them permanently, but for the present they have them. Some Spaniards regret this, but say it was the price they had to pay to vanquish Russia.

General Franco's supporters are generally so engrossed in the domestic struggle they hardly think of European apprehensions, of which almost nothing is published. Many ask why the democracies did not help General Franco defeat the "Reds" instead of letting the fascist powers do so. The widespread impression in Franco's Spain—an impression which propaganda has intensified—is that the only menace to Europe is the "Reds," and consequently the Fascist powers are working for peace. One hears this argument dozens of times, although some believe German and Italian motives in intervening in Spain were not merely a desire to check communism.

Meanwhile the triple alliance between Chancellor Adolf Hitler, Premier Benito Mussolini and General Franco is widely advertised and exalted by Insurgent propaganda. Portraits of the three dictators appear on postcards. Every hotel this traveler has seen in Rebel Spain displays German, Italian and Insurgent flags together. Mussolini's face, framed in a tin hat, glowers from the walls. Hitler's visage and book are shown in every town. The only foreign papers and magazines sold are German and Italian and one pro-Fascist London paper.

Press Hailed Hitler Visit

Hitler's visit to Rome was heralded by the Franco press in the same extravagant tones used by the Italian press about Mussolini. The Franco press, which uses foreign news selected by the German official news bureau, publishes nothing unfavorable to Hitler or Mussolini. The Pope's criticism of the Nazis in a formal letter was not published in Rebel Spain. Everything is done to make the public believe the greatest nations are fascist ones, while the democracies are feeble, decadent and outdated.

This writer asked one of the highest authorities in the Franco government what he thought would be the effect upon foreign relations of such propaganda.

"The view of the man on the street does not affect foreign relations," was his answer.

Crossing Franco Spain from Bilbao to Gibraltar, one sees Germans in every large town and some in the small ones. Some say there are only 3,000 German troops in Spain, while others say 10,000, mostly technicians and aviators. But there are many commercial agents there also.

The German soldiers are fine looking youths, with neat uniforms. They are modest and well behaved. They keep largely to themselves. Several hundred attended a bull fight in Burgos one Sunday. All of them sat together.

Hisma Is Dominant Company

The German diplomats are highly educated, well traveled and all of them speak several languages. They are well informed about Spain. The German business men are of the go-getter type which Spain may need but dislikes. The German clearing company, Hisma, has efficient and well staffed offices in half a dozen large towns from Bilbao to Seville. The Mayor of Seville said Hisma supplied almost anything the city wanted from abroad. Hisma has been the economic bulwark of the Franco movement and handled last year well over one-third of the total foreign trade in Insurgent Spain.

The Italians are less conspicuous in business. Few are seen in the large hotels in Burgos, Seville and San Sebastian, which are filled with Germans. There are said to be some 40,000 Italian soldiers sandwiched between the Spanish troops.

"That is 40,000 too many," said one Spanish officer. "Guadalajara prolonged the war a year," said another.

The Franco soldiers sing a slightly obscene song about Guadalajara and other Italian setbacks. The refrain is that Spain is not Abyssinia.

The attitude of Franco Spain toward the Germans and Italians is illustrated by the Spanish story of a barber who was shaving an Italian. The barber asked: "Why did you come here?"

The Italian replied that he came to capture Santander and Bilbao and to smash communism.

To a German who was the next customer the barber put the same question:

"I came to get shaved," said the German.

A distinguished aristocrat close to the Franco government told this writer:

"We have no commitments, political, military or economic, to Germany or Italy."

It is worth recording that British and other foreigners who have lived in Spain many years all believe that the alien forces will depart and Spain will refuse to compromise her independence.

"Our policy will be an independent one, one without alliances. We shall have had enough of war for a long time," said a specialist in foreign affairs.

"The Spanish infantry is the best in the world," said another official. "We will retain a strong army and war industries and we will be able to throw our weight about and perhaps hold the balance of power in Europe."

"When we talk of reviving the empire," said a prominent Falangist, "we mean chiefly closer cultural relations to Spanish America and the creation of a race and language like the British

Commonwealth. We have close relations to Islam, too. The Moors worship Franco. We expect soon to establish Islamic universities in Granada and Cordova. We may be able to give direction to the Mohammedan world which plays a large role in the Mediterranean."

If General Franco succeeds there probably will be a strong military dictatorship in Spain for many years. It will not want war, but it will be based on a nationalistic movement seeking greater power and prestige for Spain and having ideological affinities with fascist powers.

The Casado Coup
in Madrid

MADRID, MARCH 6, *39*

THE REPUBLICAN government of Premier Juan Negrin was super-
seded last night by a National Defense Council headed by General Segismundo Casado, Commander in Chief of the army in the
Madrid zone.

In a manifesto denouncing Premier Negrin and his colleagues
"for their evident incapacity" the council declared that "we shall
resist to the utmost limit."

The seizure of control was effected peaceably. Madrid was calm
early today.

Dr. Negrin was overthrown a few hours after he had issued a
decree transferring to himself the command of the five Republican
armies and of all to be organized in the future. Under Dr. Negrin's
decree Colonel Francisco Galan was made commander of the
naval base at Cartagena, where Nationalists attempted an uprising yesterday morning.

From the *New York Times,* March 6, 1939, copyright © 1939, 1967 by
The New York Times Company.

[Although the Nationalists reported that the uprising at Cartagena had been successful, neutral sources supported Republican contentions that it had failed.]

Miaja Supports Council

The new National Defense Council is supported by the army, Socialists, Left Republicans and Anarchists. It has the support of General José Miaja, Commander in Chief of all Republican forces under the Negrin regime.

On it the Socialists are represented by Julian Besteiro and Eduardo Valls, the Left Republicans by Miguel San Andres, the Socialist General Union of Workers by Wenceslao Carrillo and the Anarcho-Syndicalist Workers Confederation by Señor Gonzales Marin. Señor Besteiro, who is a well-known moderate Socialist leader, represented Spain at the coronation of King George VI of Britain.

In its manifesto the new council declared that "the gravity of the moment compels us to no longer obey this handful of men in whom we have no confidence." It added that members of the Negrin government had been preparing to flee abroad but that steps were taken to prevent their leaving.

"We cannot allow a privileged few quietly to make their escape to foreign countries," the statement added. "Negrin said, 'Let us stand or fall together.' Very well, so let it be. We shall resist to the utmost limit. Spaniards, long live Spain!"

Demands "a Spanish Peace"

After the statement had been broadcast General Casado declared:

"We shall resist until we are able to sign an honorable peace. The people of Spain are struggling for their independence and they will continue to struggle until such a peace is offered them. We want a Spanish peace or a fight to the finish. Spaniards, long live the Republic! Long live Spain!"

An explanation of the formation of the National Defense Council was given by Señor Besteiro in a broadcast early today.

"The time has come after a long silence," he said, "to rend the heavy tissue of lies and proclaim the truth about the Republic in a supreme effort to save the country. The truth is that after the Ebro battles the Nationalist armies occupied Catalonia and the government started wandering. The truth is that when the Ministers decided to return they lacked legality and prestige.

"The resignation of President Azaña left the Republic without a head. Under the present circumstances it is impossible constitutionally to fill the vacancy."

Señor Besteiro declared that the army "stands firm and holds the solution in its hands." Then he added:

"With veiled truths Negrin cannot aspire to gain time while time is being lost for the people in the hope that international complications will bring about a general war in which we shall all perish."

In another broadcast this morning the Madrid radio declared that the Republican zone had been "forsaken" by the Negrin government. It added that the National Defense Council assumed full responsibility for the administration of Republican Spain and was exercising full authority.

The Negrin Ministers forfeited their rights when they crossed into France after the conquest of Catalonia, the broadcast declared. The statement added:

"It is essential that in defeat we should show our moral strength. The moral victory that the Republicans might yet win would be worth more than a peace gained with limping concessions."

Only yesterday meetings were being held in Madrid, Valencia, Almeria and other strategic points, pledging support to Dr. Negrin for carrying on the war.

In his decree taking over command of the Republican armies, which was published yesterday in the Official Gazette of the Ministry of Defense, Dr. Negrin said:

"I have decided to dissolve the present organization of the armies and of the central and southern zones. The present five armies and such as may be constituted henceforth will be directly subordinated to my authority through the intermediacy of the general staff."

General Casado, who was promoted from the rank of colonel on Feb. 25, declared this morning that he was still a colonel because he considered his promotion by the Negrin government illegal.

Part 4

FOREIGN REPERCUSSIONS

ALL THE GREAT powers sailing the Mediterranean, in particular England, France, and Italy, were concerned about ways in which the Spanish Civil War might affect the balance of power in that sea. In addition, the industries, mines, telephones, and port and naval facilities in both Republican and Nationalist Spain were largely the property of foreign investors, as Lansing Warren's article ably shows. Naval incidents occurred throughout the war, but the most important and dramatic ones took place in the summer of 1937. As of April 19 the great powers, acting through the Nonintervention Committee in London, established a naval patrol of the entire Spanish coastline. Over the protest of the Republican government, Italy and Germany were assigned as so-called neutrals to patrol the coast of the Republican zone. The government warned that it would feel free to attack such ships in territorial waters. On May 29 Republican aviators bombed the *Deutschland* in Ibiza harbor, and on May 31 the Germany navy shelled the port of Almería in reprisal. Germany accused the Soviets of causing the incident, and the Franco government saw the bombing as a desperate effort by Valencia to cause a general European war in the face of sure defeat by the Nationalists. No one, however, really wanted a wider war. The Germans themselves pronounced the incident "closed" after they had shelled Almería. But they and their Axis ally, Italy, also announced their withdrawal from the naval patrol. While Britain attempted to mollify German feelings, Italy stepped up her secret submarine attacks in the Mediterranean. On August 29 "unidentified submarines" sank two Russian freighters, and on September 1 a third. Mussolini's audacity was too much for the British. It was one thing for the Axis openly to arm the Insurgents, it was another for Italy to act as a law unto herself in international waters of great consequence to England. The British called a conference of all countries bordering the Mediterranean, and in Nyon, Switzerland, it took them less than thirty-six hours (despite the ostentatious absence of Italy) to make their policy clear. They announced that the French and British navies would together patrol the entire Mediterranean, and that any unidentified submarine would risk being sunk on sight. After Nyon nothing more was heard of unidentified submarines, but also very few Russian ships sailed for Spain after August 1937. So that in fact both England and Italy got what they most wanted. Britain had acted firmly as a Mediterranean naval power; Italy had largely cut off Russian aid to the Republic, and England had, by her silence, signaled to Italy that she did not object to open Italian aid to the Nationalists.

Foreign Stakes Big in Spain

by Lansing Warren

PARIS.

ONE OF THE principal factors delaying the settlement of the war in Spain is the international complication arising from foreign investments in that country. Nearly all the key industries in Spain are controlled by foreign capital and nearly all the great powers and some of the lesser ones in Europe are eager to safeguard old concessions and investments or to acquire new ones when the final liquidation of the Spanish civil war is made.

This fact has always interposed in the negotiations for neutrality and non-intervention and in the efforts for securing peace.

Outside nations with the greatest financial interests in Spain are Great Britain, France and Germany, while Belgium and Italy have considerable stakes there. Russia and some other countries are undoubtedly contenders for whatever plums may be available.

Huge Total Involved

Spanish tax statistics put the total of foreign capital invested in Spanish industries at 1,277,000,000 gold pesetas ($417,195,900). Experts, however, say the true figure should be at least double that amount.

Great Britain is credited with holding 53.9 per cent of the total and France with 34.5—a combined total of 88.4 per cent. Much of the foreign investment, however, even when supposedly British or French, is in reality camouflaged through the medium of international consortiums so that it is impossible to trace the origin of funds, and Germany is thought to hold a much larger share in Spanish business affairs than would appear on the surface. Through the same kind of international investments Italy's part is also thought to be fairly large.

American financial interests are considered comparatively slight, except for the participation of some American bankers in international financing groups. They are believed to be limited to the control of the International Telephone and Telegraph Company, which purchased the Compania Telefonica de Espana from the Spanish State in 1924. The materials are supplied by the Standard Electrica, which is affiliated with the Standard Electric Corporation of the United States and the International General Electric Corporation. The latter concern has an interest in the Sociedad Iberica de Construcciones Electricas, which is now engaged in the electrification of the Spanish railways.

Zaharoff's Activities

The late Sir Basil Zaharoff at one time was active in Spain and is said to have obtained large orders for the Electric Boat Company of America. Vickers-Armstrong and John Brown, Ltd., of Great Britain obtained control of the Sociedad Espanola de Construccion Naval, with a capital of 60,000,000 pesetas, operating steel plants at Reinosa, navy yards at El Ferrol, Cartagena, Matagorda and Bilbao, and munitions works at La Carraca and Reinosa. In this company British financiers are collaborating with numerous wealthy Spaniards of the monarchist régime. The British stockholders do not possess a majority of the stock, but since Vickers and John Brown provide a technical guarantee for the Spanish company they do have an effective control.

Many foreign banks and holding companies are active in Spain. One of the holding companies, the Chade, or Compania Hispano-Americana de Electricidad of Barcelona, illustrates how German capital has maintained itself in Spain in camouflaged form.

The company was openly German when it was organized in 1898 by Arthur von Gwinner with the cooperation of the Deutsche Bank and the AEG (Allgemeine Elektrizität Gesellschaft) of Berlin. This company operated electric power concessions in Spain and South America, notably in Argentina. After the World War, however, Mr. von Gwinner ostensibly disposed of his interests and sold the stock to an international group, supposedly Belgian and Swiss.

A Mixed Board

The Deutsche Bank continued to be represented on the board by Georg Solmssen and the AEG by a Mr. Bucher, who was also connected with Krupp, and the Belgian board member was Dannie Heinemann, formerly AEG representative in Brussels. There was also Elkan Heinemann of Paris, who had been a collaborator of von Gwinner's. It has lately been charged that since the civil war the board of the Chade met in special session and transferred the majority of the securities to Argentina for safety.

The mining industry of Spain is mostly in the hands of the British, French and Belgians. There are a great many small companies, but very few of them are wholly Spanish, and the greater part of the mineral wealth of Spain is exploited by the big foreign companies.

First and foremost among them is the Rio Tinto Company, Ltd., of London, whose stock is almost exclusively in British hands. It has a capital stock of nearly £4,000,000, reserves of £1,500,000 and stock issues of about £2,000,000.

The Bombing of the Deutschland —by Six Reporters

SOVIET PLOT IS SEEN IN BERLIN

By Eugene J. Young

REALISTIC ASSESSORS of war possibilities have been saying for weeks that the Spanish civil war—tragic as it is—has been healthy for Europe. German and Italian advocates of conquest have tried out the methods and weapons with which they had calculated to gain quick victories on larger fields. They found that, even with a badly hampered defense, swift triumph was impossible and, if they were to take on more formidable foes, they had to calculate on being ready for a long struggle.

Evidence that they have learned the lesson is given by the swiftness with which the latest crisis was put in process of liquidation. There was a chance for a real conflagration. Armed forces had clashed, and prestige was involved because warships of both Germany and Italy had come off badly in contacts with Spanish bombing planes. Judged by the time taken to abate the scares over the German repudiation of the Versailles treaty and the reoccupation of the Rhineland, it might have been expected that many days, perhaps weeks, would be consumed in fulminations and threats, if not serious direct action.

Haste in Ending Tension

Under these circumstances, the haste shown by the statesmen in Berlin and Rome in ending the tension is highly enlightening. The German dictatorship, it is true, felt compelled to do something drastic to cover the wound to its prestige; and something drastic was done in the bombardment of Almeria. Yet it is to be noted that the port chosen for the demonstration was one poorly equipped with coast defenses and airplanes, so there was small chance of a Spanish reaction which might have forced further conflict; and the warships withdrew quickly. Then Berlin swiftly announced that the affair was ended.

Mussolini refrained from taking any direct action in retaliation for the bombing of Italy's warship. He gave warning that Italian ships would fire on any Spanish ships or planes which appeared to threaten them. Beyond that he contented himself with notice that Russian ships would not be permitted to carry supplies to the Loyalist government. In view of the fact that his navy had been accused of cooperating for months in an effective blockade against such Soviet activities, this new order did little to worsen the situation.

Berlin, for its part, went out of the way to placate British opinion and to set under way again the process of finding a path toward economic and financial accords that might ease its home strains. Rome was more offish, but indicated it was willing to listen to reason.

Democracies Remain Calm

The calm unity of the democracies undoubtedly had its effect on the adventurous ones. France, now firmly assured of solidarity with Britain, from the first pooh-poohed the danger of a general war as

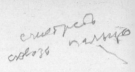

a result of the bombing of the Deutschland. This poise was in sharp contrast to the apprehension over the Rhineland incident.

Britain coolly warned Germany against going too far. Ambassador von Ribbentrop was called to the Foreign Office, and there Secretary Eden pointedly abjured his country not to take any action which would add to the gravity of a situation already grave. Then London statesmanship set out to patch up the anti-intervention front and to give the dictatorships an opportunity to "save face" without resorting to inflammatory activities.

In the face of a rapidly rearming Britain and a strengthened France which was continuing to cooperate closely with London on European affairs, it became quite plain that any adventuring might prove disastrous. This was especially so in the case of nations badly strained economically and financially and therefore not able to contemplate a long struggle.

Another factor which swayed Berlin was set forth in dispatches from that capital. There was a strong suspicion that the Soviet was deliberately trying to bring on a general war in Western Europe so that Germany might be crushed, or at least badly crippled, by Britain and France before she was ready for a grand campaign eastward.

Some writers charged that the responsibility for the Deutschland affair lay with the Russian air force and that it had deliberately launched an attack in the belief that the Reich would be compelled to take such drastic measures as would embroil all the great powers in the West. The theory had a basis of plausibility. Russia might gain much in such a war. She could take advantage of it for an advance into Poland, Central Europe or the Balkans; or she might remain aloof in the West and take advantage of the weaknesses developing in Japan.

Aid from Britain

At any rate, Berlin would not play into the hands of its great coming adversary. And in taking this position it had aid from Britain. That nation hastened to show the Spanish Government— and the Russians in the background—that she would not be made a catspaw for Soviet chestnuts. She made clear that she did not condone the bombing of the Deutschland and served notice she would not join in measures to prevent such incidents in future by evolving the plan for a four-power front to deal with them.

If there were any suppositions that the visit of Field Marshal von Blomberg to Rome was to bring about fresh intervention in Spain they were not based on sound premises. The German army chief at this moment is a pacificator rather than a war-maker. He knows that his country is far from being ready for trouble.

Because of the activity of the German airplanes in Spain, particularly on the Bilbao front in recent weeks, there is a misconception of the German involvement in the civil war. The army chiefs are not yet fully in control of the air forces. Colonel-General Goering, the second figure in the Nazi hierarchy, has kept his hold on them and it is he who sent the planes to Spain for what the French charge is a "rehearsal" for the war of terror and destruction he intends to wage on others when the time comes.

Blomberg's Stand

Accounts from Spain agree that German participation in other military fields has been limited. Blomberg has opposed involvement of the German Army. And doubtless Mussolini has found him still of that mind and therefore has received small encouragement for any plans for joint action to smash the Loyalists.

On the other side of the world also there has been a distinct check to military adventurers. The reorganization of the Japanese Cabinet is a victory—limited but real—for the moderate forces which are now seeking accord rather than strife.

The main issues lay in the determination of the army to smash the parliamentary system by ignoring the political parties in setting up an inner government which should be ruled by it and in its designs to subject all the nation's affairs to close control in the interest of war-making. But Emperor Hirohito has again intervened in behalf of the Diet. Its parties lack full recognition in the Cabinet of Prince Konoe, but leaders of them are included in the Ministry. Also, Konoe has served notice that the Cabinet is to represent the whole country and that he will not permit domination by any group.

Foreign affairs are again to be entrusted to Hirota, close friend of the Emperor. He has long fought the militarists and has several times given pledges that the nation shall not go to war while he is in authority.

FASCIST AND COMMUNIST POWERS DRAW BACK FROM A WAR OVER SPAIN

By Arnaldo Cortesi

ROME, JUNE 5.

ONE OF THE most incomprehensible of many incomprehensible points about the air attack on the Deutschland May 29 is why the Valencia government thought it worthwhile to resort to an action the only possible result of which could have been to cement the friendship of Italy and Germany—General Francisco Franco's two main supporters—and render it more difficult for them to abandon the Spanish enterprise.

Both Italy and Germany had been lending last week, and had been lending for some time, an attentive ear to the suggestions emanating from the London Foreign Office for a compromise solution of the Spanish civil war, but both would sooner continue fighting than have the appearance of being thrown out of Spanish territory instead of leaving of their own free will.

The Deutschland bombing is even stranger because the policy of the Valencia government no less than France's Popular Front and the Soviet's has been directed to driving a wedge between Italy and Germany.

It has not escaped observers here, for instance, that Julio Alvarez del Vayo's indictment of the Fascist government in Geneva did not mention Germany at all, and it had the evident purpose of dividing Italy and Germany. When on the 24th and 26th of last month Italian ships were bombed while German ships were spared, it looked as if the same policy were being continued.

Then came the Deutschland attack, which was a complete undoing of whatever success Valencia had in fostering the disparity of views between Premier Benito Mussolini and Chancellor Adolf Hitler about Spain.

Rome and Berlin Closer

Last week's events had the effect of strengthening the Rome-Berlin axis at the very point where it had given some evidence of being the weakest. It was no secret, in fact, that Mussolini and Hitler did not see quite eye to eye in the Spanish situation, which was clearly brought out during Foreign Minister Constantin von Neurath's recent Rome visit. It was quite evident that Germany wanted to abandon the Spanish enterprise just as soon as could be done without too severe a loss of dignity, whereas Italy favored making one more effort to bring about a military solution of the war.

Whatever the ultimate result of the Deutschland affair may be, its immediate effect cannot help but make Germany more inclined to fall in with the Italian view—that it is necessary to take at least one good swipe at the Valencia government's forces.

The bombing of Italian and German warships has decreased, but it has not destroyed, the possibility of a compromise solution of the civil war. There is every reason to believe that Mussolini is still not averse to listening to the proposals Foreign Secretary Anthony Eden is making, and the only thing he wants is some sufficiently glamorous success to enable him to withdraw from Spain with the halo of victory around his brow. The fact that Hitler restricted his reprisals for the Deutschland attack indicates that he also does not wish to push matters to extreme consequences.

Defense Held Stronger

This attitude on both Italy's and Germany's part is a result of the severity the fighting in Spain is assuming increasingly as each month passes. Defending troops have had time to dig in thoroughly, and it is obvious that military operations on a very large scale will be necessary to dislodge them. This conclusion is also reached by the slowness with which the Bilbao offensive is progressing. General Franco's troops in almost two months have succeeded in advancing only a score or so of miles on a very limited front.

Bilbao may or may not fail in the more or less distant future, but it has in any case already proved that the advantage in modern warfare is all with the defenders and that the attackers cannot hope to win unless they have a crushing superiority of men and materials.

Either Italy or Germany probably would settle the Spanish conflict without much difficulty if they were willing to undertake a real war. They would face, however, considerable losses of men, and the question arises whether the final results would justify the sacrifice of many thousands of lives. The conviction seems to be gaining ground that it would not.

By Guido Enderis

BERLIN, JUNE 5.

RECENT EVENTS in Spanish waters have afforded a fresh demonstration of the promptness with which the now familiar political contrivance known as the Berlin-Rome axis can be requisitioned whenever Italo-German interests call for collaboration.

Since its introduction last Autumn into the complicated mechanism of European politics, the axis steadily has been galvanized into a political instrument over which Chancellor Hitler can dispose with the same freedom as Premier Mussolini. The axis can be set in motion at the precise moment either dictator deems it opportune.

The promptness with which the Italians walked out of the London Non-Intervention Committee after the Reich's exit following the bombing of the Deutschland and the bombardment of Almeria constituted a wholly spontaneous action, it is declared here. As such, it must be accepted as concrete proof that the Berlin and Rome governments see eye to eye in respect to Spain as well as all other problems that come within the range of their paralleling interests.

The Axis Formed

As a political conception the axis is of comparatively recent origin. It became an influential factor in European politics following the visit of Count Ciano, the Italian Foreign Minister, to Chancellor Hitler at Berchtesgaden last Autumn. That visit produced the so-called Berchtesgaden protocols providing for active consultation between Berlin and Rome on all matters affecting their common interests.

Both governments were then already deeply involved in the Spanish civil crisis.

Revolutions of the Berlin-Rome axis, it is asseverated, are not designed to project a discordant note into the European concert. They are intended to impress upon other nations animated by good will that democracies can sit in peace at the same table with dictatorships. But thus far there has been no indication that the Soviet dictators are wanted at this table, and there is considerable evidence that the axis partners do not propose to permit the Soviets to get a foothold in Western Europe.

The ceremonious reception accorded Field Marshal von Blomberg in Rome during the past week, no less than the hospitality extended to General Goering on the occasion of his recent visit to Italy, must be accepted as evidence that communications between Berlin and Rome continue to function smoothly.

Spanish incidents, if anything, have brought both regimes into more intimate contact.

With political ties becoming more firmly knotted, it is desirable, say German officials, that expression also be given to closer relations of the armed forces of the two countries, just as they are working toward fuller cooperation in the economic field.

By Harold Denny

MOSCOW, JUNE 5.

VIGILIS, THE Kremlin's journalistic spokesman, thundered heavily and repeatedly in Izvestia this week against Fascist activities in Spain, which, in Soviet eyes, reached their climax of high-handedness in the bombardment of Almeria by a German naval squadron. Thus far, however, there is no indication that the Soviet will do more in this new crisis than try to stiffen the attitude of Great Britain and France.

To the question of whether the Soviet Union is willing to go to war against fascism the answer, at this period, at any rate, is definitely "no." The Soviet Government wants more than anything else to keep out of external trouble, even though it is greatly concerned at the mounting power and aggressiveness of states governed by communism's rival panacea.

Government and Red Army leaders are constantly reiterating that their armament is purely for defense. That statement is literally true now for several reasons.

Still in Experiment

The most important of these is that the Soviet Union is still in the throes of an enormous experiment that would be disturbed even by a victorious war. And Soviet leaders, although continually expressing full confidence of the ability of the Red Army to repulse any combination of powers that might engage it, would rather not see the country involved in a war in which Russia, with a still vastly inadequate transport system, would almost certainly have to fight powerful armies on both the west and the east.

Furthermore, the whole Soviet organism is now undergoing a searching for "spies" and "wreckers." It is dismissing, arresting, demoting and transferring executives and engineers under various charges from Trotskyism to inefficiency.

The government is even shaking up the Red Army, establishing a system of military councils to take command of each military district, thus lessening the authority of individual commanders. This is doubly not the time for the Soviet to become involved in any external war.

Then, too, even if the Soviet Union wanted to try conclusions with the Fascist powers, how could she?

Navy Powerless to Act

There was a great outcry here last December when a Spanish Rebel warship sank the Soviet merchantman Comsomol. Demands were made then that the Red Navy convoy every Soviet ship bound for Spain. But that was not done for the reason that the Red Navy, although planning a capital ship program, at present consists largely of destroyers, gunboats and submarines, useful only for coast defense. The Soviet Union simply could not engage in serious naval activity off the Spanish coast.

At best it will be years before the Soviet Union can have a strong, far-ranging navy. Without such a navy, the geographical situation seems to preclude the possibility of sending an expeditionary force to Spain, even if Russia wished.

Confronted by what they consider the genuine menace of fascism, the Communists employ subtler tactics with some success. It was the rising tide of fascism that caused the Comintern to shift its position radically two years ago and to seek to enlist radicals, Socialists and liberals into a united front in opposition to the spread of fascism. From abusing these elements as the worst enemies of communism on the ground that they would palliate the evils of capitalism, thus enabling it to survive, instead of boldly planning its overthrow, they turned to wooing them as necessary allies against fascism. The Spanish Government, now fighting for its life, is one of the products of these changed tactics.

The Kremlin appears still to hope that something may come out of the London Non-Intervention Committee, even though the committee has suspended its sessions and, in the Soviet view, has been largely ineffectual.

SPANISH FOES UNSHAKEN BY SETBACKS

By William P. Carney

SALAMANCA, SPAIN, JUNE 5.

UNTIL GENERAL Emilio Mola's death in an airplane accident plunged the Nationalists [Insurgents] into mourning, they jubilantly viewed the week's earlier events as foreshadowing "the beginning of the end" of the war.

However, they say their military machine is still more than strong enough to withstand the loss of even so valuable a general as the commander of their northern army.

In the opinion of officials here, only a desire on the part of the Valencia government to provoke a European war as a final desperate effort to avoid complete defeat explains the bombing by Valencia's planes first of an Italian warship and then of the German pocket battleship Deutschland, which was assigned to the non-intervention patrol of Spain's Mediterranean coast.

Bombing Held Justified

The subsequent bombardment of Almeria by the German pocket battleship Admiral Scheer as a reprisal is regarded in Salamanca as thoroughly justified, and the fact that Britain and France are making strenuous efforts to pacify both Italy and Germany and persuade them to return to the non-intervention committee is taken as an indication that the British Foreign Office and the Quai d'Orsay are both extremely anxious to sidestep the war danger.

Barcelona disturbances and the general Catalan situation, coupled with the military reverses on the Basque and Madrid fronts after the loss of Malaga in February, brought the downfall of the Largo Caballero government. Less than a fortnight later its successor, the Negrin Cabinet, signified its intention of resigning as soon as assurances had been obtained that a new government could be formed. Thus far Julian Besteiro and Diego Martinez Barrio have been unable to fulfill the mission that President Manuel Azana asked them to undertake.

This correspondent can testify as a witness to military failures of the Valencia Government forces in the past week. The Nationalist attacks began early last Sunday morning. By Thursday General José Miaja's forces had already suffered 3,000 casualties, of which 1,000 killed were counted.

In Summer Heat

In blazing heat—the temperature in Central Spain is already as high as it goes in midsummer—the writer stood in the middle of the highway leading to Corunna, five miles from Madrid's Puerta del Sol, and watched shells falling into the city. This point, on the Cuesta de las Perdices, is marked by a milestone which reads Kilometer 8, and is exactly opposite Cubas Villa, which the Madrid radio announced falsely that government forces had captured last week.

In a tour of the entire Madrid front with General Franco's staff officers I also visited the clinical building in University City and was able to verify that General Franco's troops there were not isolated. The commanding officer in this sector said they had never been cut off from the rest of the Nationalist forces in the Casa de Campo or Pozuelo and Aravaca.

Since last Monday fires and electric lights have been observed in Madrid for the first time since last November, and shooting at night in the streets has been heard. Prisoners taken by the Nationalists say there is nightly fighting between the Syndicalist and Socialist trade unionists.

Last Sunday was the twenty-fifth anniversary of the dedication of the Sacred Heart Monument on the Hill of the Angels a few miles south of Madrid, which is the exact geographic center of the Iberian peninsula.

The monument, a statue of Christ, was a gift from former King Alfonso. It was dynamited at the outbreak of the civil war and the site was renamed Red Hill in a decree signed by former Premier Francisco Largo Caballero. It was recaptured by General Franco's forces November 5 and has never been taken since by the Loyalists, although I was told by the commanding officers there that the enemy had reached the esplanade one day at the end of last January and remained for three hours until Nationalists drove them away.

By Herbert L. Matthews

MADRID, JUNE 5.

EUROPE PROBABLY has had no more critical moment since the World War ended than the Valencia Cabinet meeting Monday morning, after German warships had bombarded Almeria.

If the Loyalists had been in a desperate military situation and had seen no hope of relief except by provoking Germany and precipitating a European war, nothing could have been easier. Fortunately for all concerned, the Valencia government had every interest in preventing such a development. Hence the worst of the excitement is now over.

The incident, however, is destined to leave its mark. It may be closed, but it cannot be forgotten. It is bound to have a profound effect on the course of the civil war.

As far as its judicial aspect is concerned, there is no apparent solution, although the Valencia government considers its case clear-cut. As the Loyalists see it, the German pocket battleship Deutschland had no right to be in Iviza harbor in the Balearic Islands and less right to open fire without warning on two Spanish Government planes flying above it, as the Loyalists insist the warship did. It is argued that the bombing was therefore justified, whereas the shelling of Almeria was by the same token a case of unjustified aggression against a sovereign power.

Sympathy for Germany

Nevertheless, as the House of Commons debate in London Tuesday demonstrated, world opinion will sweep aside the merely judicial aspect and concentrate on the fact that since several of the Deutschland's sailors were killed or wounded, Germany had a right to feel aggrieved. The fact that Spain also has a grievance is acknowledged as well, and the whole incident is dismissed as deplorable.

Of course one cannot expect Spaniards in Loyalist territory to see the controversy in that light. The attitude that the entire Loyalist press has taken, for instance, is this: "Germany is waging war against us without declaring it."

There are many more bitter sentiments to that effect. Popular reaction was more sentimental, even more bitter. What seemingly infuriated the man in the street was not the fact that Germany retaliated for the Deutschland bombing but the way she retaliated. If a Loyalist warship had been bombed in return, for instance, the revenge would at least have seemed logical to Spaniards. But what they couldn't stomach was the bombardment of a defenseless port.

The only consolation drawn from the incident by the Loyalists is the belief that if Germany did have a case before world opinion, she threw it away by her action.

There was no place for sentiment as far as the Valencia Cabinet was concerned. It is known now that one factor dominated all others: the civil war must be permitted to continue as a civil war and not as a part of a European war. The Valencia government wants nothing else so much as to be let alone to carry on. For the government and all Loyalists say they are certain that they are going to win the war on the present basis.

Bitter Pill Swallowed

Such being the case, the last thing they want is to goad Germany— and Italy—into a far greater degree of intervention on General Francisco Franco's side. There is a bitter pill to swallow, but the evidence now is that it will be swallowed in the paramount interest of winning the war.

That is the policy behind the government's action this week. But of course, things will not continue just as if the Almeria incident had not occurred.

In the first place, every Loyalist is convinced that Germany and Italy will use the affair for the twofold purpose of strengthening their blockade against the Spanish coast and at the same time as a cloak for further, even though still limited, intervention. Therefore the government's reaction will be a speeding up of its plans to take the offensive this Summer.

It has become more than ever imperative either to put a quick end to the war or at least to gain some solid victories to justify before the world the confidence the Loyalists feel in themselves. So the Iviza and Almeria incidents have set things in motion that must affect the war's course profoundly. However, there is no need to worry about a European war, as far as the Valencia government is concerned.

Dealing with Mediterranean Piracy

AT NYON

THE LITTLE SWISS town of Nyon on Lake Geneva was host last week to the latest of European conferences, called to meet the deepening diplomatic crisis born of the Spanish civil war. Nyon, but fourteen miles from Geneva where the League Council met in brief session last Friday, clusters on a hillside crowned with a sixteenth-century castle from which can be seen the blue waters of the lake and distant, snow-capped Mont Blanc. The diplomats had little time for scenery. They were occupied with the peace of Europe.

The crisis before them arose in the Mediterranean. For months merchant ships, many of them bound for Loyalist Spain, have been subject to mysterious submarine attacks, bombing from the air, shelling by unidentified warships. The Loyalists, aware that the Insurgents have but few submarines, accused Italy of the attacks. The charge was on the League Council's agenda last week. Other powers marked time until ten days ago the British destroyer

From the *New York Times,* September 12, 1937, copyright © 1937, 1965 by The New York Times Company.

Havock narrowly missed torpedoing. Britain was stung to action.

Franco-British Bid

With the support of France, invitations were sent to ten powers for "immediate consultation and action . . . now become necessary in order to deal with the intolerable situation created by attacks recently illegally carried out against shipping in the Mediterranean by submarines and airplanes without disclosure of their identity."

Acceptances were received from Russia, Greece, Egypt, Rumania, Bulgaria, Yugoslavia and Turkey. Three nations declined: Italy, Albania (the country is dominated by Italy) and Germany. Behind their refusal lay another diplomatic crisis—a threatened rupture of Italo-Russian relations.

Russia and Italy, until the war in Ethiopia, were good friends. Italy was early to recognize the Soviets, and at a conference in Genoa in 1922 made it possible for Soviet statesmen for the first time to meet foreign diplomats on equal terms. Later Italy became an important market for Russian oil. Four years ago the two countries signed a non-aggression pact.

Friendship faded when Italy invaded Ethiopia. It died when Italy sided with the Spanish Insurgents, for Russian sympathies were with the Government at Valencia.

Soviet Ships Sunk

Two Russian merchant ships were recently sunk by submarines in the Mediterranean. Last week in an unexpected and strongly worded note the Soviet Union, claiming to have "indubitable proofs of aggressive actions of Italian warships," blamed Italy for the loss of the Russian vessels. The Russians characterized the sinkings as in "flagrant contravention not only of the principles of humanity but of the most elementary and generally recognized precepts of international law." Discontinuance of the attacks, as well as compensation for the damage done, was insisted upon.

Italy replied: "The Italian Government denies the responsibility [for the sinkings] even as it rejects the Soviet demands en bloc." A second Soviet protest was then dispatched to Rome.

In Russia, while these exchanges were in progress, the press was demanding that a firm hand be taken with Italy. The Red Star, organ of the army, declared that the Soviet Government would "find the necessary means for calling the sea pirates to their responsibility and forcing them to fulfill the demands of the Soviet note."

The sudden quarrel between Italy and the Soviet Union—the Soviet protest arrived almost at the same time as the invitation to the Nyon meeting—had an inevitable reaction on the Italian attitude toward the proposed parley. "It is impossible to sit at the same table with such people," said an official at the Italian Foreign Office.

Wires along the Rome-Berlin axis hummed. (Actually it was the Rome-Nuremberg axis, since Chancellor Hitler and all important German officials were in Nuremberg for the annual Nazi party congress.) Germany and Italy, already linked by understandings, maintained their common front.

Italo-German Refusal

In almost identical notes delivered simultaneously they refused to go to Nyon, basing their stand on the Russian protests. They accused the other powers of unwillingness to act at the time of the alleged attempt to torpedo the German cruiser Leipzig last June. (Last May, in retaliation for the alleged Loyalist bombing of the Deutschland, German warships bombarded the Loyalist port of Almeria.) They suggested that the whole subject of so-called piracy in the Mediterranean be referred to the Non-Intervention Committee, organized a year ago in the hope of maintaining European peace by preventing the powers from aiding either side in the Spanish struggle.

Though Italian and German refusals had been forecast, and those two nations believed their absence would wreck the Nyon conference, Britain and France went ahead with plans for the parley. In preparation the British Cabinet met for the first time since July. As 10 Downing Street was being redecorated, the Ministers gathered at 2 Whitehall Gardens, once the home of Disraeli.

The Cabinet selected a strong delegation: Foreign Secretary Anthony Eden; Sir Robert Vansittart, permanent head of the Foreign Office; Admiral Sir Alfred Ernle Montacute Chatfield, First Sea Lord. The membership revealed British belief in the importance of the meeting. But that Britain did not believe the situation yet acute was indicated by Prime Minister Chamberlain's departure after the Cabinet meeting for fishing in Scotland.

Last Friday the diplomats gathered at Nyon. Last night, after prolonged debate in which the other powers sought to soothe Russia's ruffled feelings, they reached an accord. It provided that Britain and France would supervise sea lanes throughout the Mediterranean. All at Nyon would be responsible for their own territorial waters, although Russia would have special control of the Black Sea and would have the right to send her warships into the Mediterranean if necessary to protect her merchant vessels.

Awaits Approval

The accord was referred to the home governments for approval, after which the diplomats will meet again. Italy was invited to support the control scheme, but in Rome it was said that acceptance might be conditioned on recognition of belligerent rights for the Insurgents.

In an effort to keep sea lanes open for supply ships the Spanish Loyalist navy was reported to have engaged the Insurgent naval forces. Supplies, particularly oil, are regarded as essential if the Loyalists are to keep up their fight. Last week the Aragon front, recently the scene of a Loyalist offensive, appeared to be quiet following the reported Loyalist capture of Belchite, an important link in Insurgent communications between Saragossa and Teruel. On the Bay of Biscay front, despite stout Asturian resistance, the Insurgents moved steadily toward Gijon, the last important Loyalist city in that region.

AGREEMENT REACHED AT NYON

By P. J. Philip

NYON, SWITZERLAND, SEPT. 11.

WITH SIXTY destroyers, 40 per cent of which will be French, and with an air fleet in about the same proportion, the French and British Navy chiefs today assured the Nyon Conference for the Suppression of Piracy in the Mediterranean that they can rid that sea of its pests and re-establish law and order.

From the conference they got these instructions: That they should counter-attack and if possible destroy any submarine attacking any merchant ship not belonging to either party in the Spanish conflict.

So within less than thirty-six hours of its opening this conference reached a definite result. Its decisions must await the formal ratification by the powers concerned, but the signature of the agreement is expected by Wednesday at the latest and by the next week-end the largest fleet of destroyers ever assembled in that sea will begin clearing the Mediterranean of its phantom pirates.

Zone Offered to Italy

Of course the big burden falls on the French and British. Other riparian countries decided they could not do more than protect their territorial waters and offer the hospitality of their ports. In that decision there was this advantage: It excluded Soviet Russia from participation, control and protection in the Mediterranean and made it possible for the conference to offer the control of the Tyrrhenian Sea to Italy.

But as the conference formally refused to acknowledge the belligerent rights of either party in the Spanish war it is almost certain that Italy will not accept. Whether she does or does not

France and Britain will go ahead with their plans and their instructions.

These are set forth in two communiqués summarizing fully the agreements which had been reached in the three-hour conference in the Nyon municipal assembly room. In the first of them some account is given of the meeting and of the proposal of the Balkan Entente made by Bozidar Pouritch, Yugoslav Minister to France, "on maritime routes which are most used and in accordance with itineraries which might be agreed upon, policing the seas to be carried out by British and French naval forces as has been agreed upon by the British and French Governments."

Other riparian nations declared that after consideration of the naval forces at their disposal they had come to the conclusion that they could not do more than protect their territorial waters.

It was not until nearly 11 o'clock tonight that the British and French delegations issued a second communiqué jointly stating what exactly had been agreed upon and giving details on the manner in which the patrol would be carried out. The statement follows.

Principal Provisions Listed

"The principal provisions of the agreement reached today are as follows:

"In the preamble it is made clear that the participating governments, in agreeing on the special collective measures to be taken against piratical acts perpetrated by submarines, do not mean to concede to either of the parties in Spain the right to exercise belligerent rights.

"The agreement provides that the naval forces of the participating powers will counterattack and, if possible, destroy any submarines attacking, contrary to the rules of international law as laid down in the London Naval Treaty of 1930, merchant ships not belonging to either party to the Spanish conflict.

"They will take the same action regarding any submarine encountered in the vicinity of the position where a merchant vessel has just been attacked in circumstances giving valid ground for believing the submarine guilty of the attack in question.

"In the Western Mediterranean and in the Malta Channel, with the exception of the Tyrrhenian Sea which may form the subject of special arrangements, the British and French fleets will give practical effect to the conference's decision. In the Eastern Mediterranean the conference's decision will be carried out, in so far as territorial waters are concerned, by riparian powers. On the high seas it will be entrusted, with the exception of the Adriatic Sea, to the British and French fleets.

"The other riparian governments will provide, so far as their means allow, such assistance as may be asked of them, and particularly will allow them the use of such of their ports as they may indicate. In order to facilitate the execution of these measures, no submarines of the participating powers will be put to sea in the Mediterranean unless accompanied by a surface vessel or in certain zones to be defined for the purpose of exercise.

"Powers will not admit entry into their respective territorial waters of any foreign submarine except in case of urgent distress or where a submarine is proceeding accompanied and on the surface. They will advise their merchant shipping to follow certain main routes in the Mediterranean, to be agreed upon between them."

Yvon Delbos, French Foreign Minister who had spent most of the night, supported by the French naval experts, explaining to other powers what was proposed and negotiating with some of them on how to get around the difficulties raised by the others, presided at this afternoon's meeting, which of course was strictly private. Most of these difficulties lay in the fact that other riparian powers could not agree what share they should take in protecting their own and each other's waters.

First, their deficiency in ships and, secondly, their reluctance to cooperate made it impossible to divide the Eastern Mediterranean into zones, so the matter was left at this: They would protect their own territorial waters and give help if and when asked by the French and the British.

It was perhaps only incidental that Soviet Russia in this way was confined to the Black Sea, but there energetic measures were promised. For the Black Sea powers had it inserted in the communiqué that should freedom of traffic in that sea be threatened from submarine action, they would immediately unite as to the steps to be taken to put an end to such activities.

Speaking for their delegations this evening, the British and French official spokesmen declared emphatically that the task and duty of the Anglo-French fleet would be to protect all merchant shipping from attack, irrespective of nationality, with the solitary exception that it would not interfere in a fight between Spanish vessels.

It was also explained that whether or not Italy accepted the offer to take over control of the Tyrrhenian, it did not make the slightest difference to the conference's decisions or action of the naval commanders, who alone would be judges as to whether there were valid grounds for the belief that a submarine had been guilty of attack and for sinking her.

Satisfaction Is Expressed

It is understood that any contracting parties to this agreement can get out of it by giving one month's notice. Otherwise it stands for the duration of the danger in the Mediterranean.

Over the speed with which this agreement was reached, and its completeness, there is tonight great satisfaction in British and French circles. That satisfaction in some cases is clouded by the doubt whether it is of advantage or otherwise to the Valencia government. The Spanish Government delegates in Geneva are especially disheartened on finding themselves treated on the same plane as Insurgents, but that issue is only incidental, in the minds of the British at least, to the protection of illegal attacks against shipping.

The phrase inserted into the communiqué's second paragraph, about submarines attacking "contrary to the rules of international law as laid down by the London Naval Treaty," by naval experts is treated somewhat as legal hair-splitting, for, it is pointed out, no submarine can do otherwise effectively, especially if it wishes to remain anonymous.

What is assured is that merely the pirates' anonymity will not protect them. If any venture into the net spread by the sixty destroyers and their vigilant airplane scouts, they will do so accompanied by a surface vessel and flying their own true colors, or risk being sunk.

When the last details of the agreement were settled, M. Delbos, in a short speech, thanked his fellow delegates for having worked so quickly and successfully. By doing so, he said, the conference has made an important contribution to the reestablishment of the law of nations, the pacification of the Mediterranean, freedom of navigation and the cause of peace, which would follow from respect for the law of nations.

What has come into being in the opinion of many is an effective Franco-British force for the defense of principles and laws to which so much lip service is paid in Geneva.

Part 5

THE DEVELOPMENT OF NATIONALIST SPAIN

FROM THE moment he took command of the army in Morocco on July 19, 1936, General Franco was determined to rebuild Spain along traditional lines. He became the uncontested political as well as military chieftain of Nationalist Spain in the spring of 1937, and after his armies reached the Mediterranean coast in April 1938 the entire world recognized him as the inevitable ruler of post–Civil War Spain. He had from the beginning enjoyed the favor of the international business community. Harold Callender's article indicates clearly how Franco traded not only with his German and Italian allies but with British, Belgian, and American firms; and how he managed to maintain a stable peseta and to boost foreign trade to the point where exports from Nationalist Spain alone in 1937 were about equal in volume to the total of

Spanish exports in 1935, the last year before the civil war. Callender's "Vignettes" indicate also the Insurgents' abundance of food (Franco held the less populated, agricultural portions of Spain) and the appearance of "normality" and of at least a surface political unity. At the same time, in his paragraph reflecting on the death of the young German flier Wilmcen, Callender anticipates the worst aspect of World War II, Korea, Vietnam . . . civilized-looking youngsters dropping explosives on defenseless civilians.

Hugh Trevor-Roper's article was written at a time when both industrial and student unrest was causing many to predict the imminent demise of the Franco regime. But the author understood the extent to which even its old opponents by 1956 considered that regime to be a guarantee against renewed civil war, and how that regime allowed for "tendencies" even while it prohibited political parties. In short, Trevor-Roper understood the personal strength of character, the political genius, and the solidly traditional basis of Franco's rule. He is correct in stating that Franco has at all times considered himself the regent of a "social and popular," not a democratic and constitutional, monarchy. The source of tantalizing doubts with Franco has not been the nature of the state he wished to leave at his retirement or death, but simply *when* he would restore a king, and *who* that king would be. Still in power fifteen years after the date of the Trevor-Roper essay, he has clarified one point, namely that Juan Carlos, grandson of Alfonso XIII, rather than the young prince's father, the Pretender Juan de Bourbon, will some day be king of Spain. But as these lines are written in 1971 the aging dictator still has not indicated when he himself expects to relinquish power.

There are a couple of minor errors to correct in Trevor-Roper's generally excellent essay. There were not two but sixteen Communist deputies (out of a total of 473) in the Popular Front Cortes. It is correct in fact to say that Franco was saving Spain from liberal democracy rather than from communism, but the "communist menace" was indeed played up very prominently in rightist manifestos both before and during the war. To write that "Spain is a part of Africa accidentally attached to Europe" is to repeat one of the oldest and most misleading of historical clichés. Spain was indeed long ruled by the Muslims, and its middle class is much weaker than those of France and northern European countries. But in modern times, at least since the mid-eighteenth century, Spain has borne much closer resemblance to Italy or France than to Morocco or Egypt.

Franco Financed Without a Loan

by Harold Callender

GIBRALTAR, MAY 13.

IN A CIVIL war now apparently entering its final stage, Nationalist [Insurgent] Spain's achievement on the economic front is hardly less remarkable than on the military front.

There has been no government loan in the ordinary sense, either internal or external. There is only one notable new tax. There was virtually no gold to draw upon, but there are other resources and the Franco movement has been financed chiefly in these ways:

First, by foreign exchange from exports, mainly of raw materials. Foreign currency has been appropriated by the Franco government, even when it belonged to foreign concerns operating in Spain. The owners have received in return at the fixed official rate Spanish pesetas blocked inside Franco Spain.

Secondly, by long-term credits from Germany and Italy for war materials and manufactured goods. These credits are guaranteed by assets outside Spain owned by wealthy Spaniards. One official said they would be repaid within ten years.

Thirdly, by gold and foreign currencies and securities held

abroad by Spaniards, but commandeered by the Franco government. These have been deposited with the government for use in making payments or as collateral for credits as British nationals' property abroad was deposited with their government in 1914. It is understood that the only foreign gilt-edged securities that have been sold are British and Argentine bonds.

Fourthly, by so-called "voluntary" gifts from rich Spaniards living abroad or in Franco Spain. Since the proclamation of the Spanish Republic in 1931 wealthy Spaniards had been moving their capital abroad. Now a share of these assets in France, Switzerland, The Netherlands and Great Britain has been given outright to the Franco Government.

Fifthly, by war industries acquired in the course of the armies' advance and war material captured on land and sea during the war.

Sixthly, by a 10 per cent tax on drinks and luxuries generally.

Seventhly, by bank notes printed in Germany for the Bank of Spain and government paper paid out for supplies and discounted at the bank.

A high official of the Nationalist Ministry of Commerce told this correspondent exports in 1937 had produced assets in sterling equal to $50,000,000 to $60,000,000. This sterling total included trade with almost all countries except Generalissimo Francisco Franco's allies. Officials of the German company, Hisma, formed to carry on clearing and trade between Germany and Spain, said that the 1937 Spanish exports thus bartered for German goods were valued at something like $31,000,000. On this evidence it would seem that Franco Spain's exports last year came to about $90,000,000 or nearly as much as the exports of the whole of Spain the year before the war, which amounted—valued in gold pesetas—to only $115,000,000. One official at Burgos said they exceeded the figure for all Spain for 1935.

Peseta's Value Agreed Upon

Clearing transactions, in addition to war material transactions, between Franco Spain and Germany, are based on the paper peseta at an agreed exchange value of 3.44 to the mark, according to a German source. It is said the Germans have received assurance that Franco Spain will not reduce this debt by devaluing its currency. There is apparently no specific agreement to this effect, for Germans do not seem too optimistic. Many holding pesetas have lately bought land and capital goods in Spain as a hedge against devaluation. Spaniards are doing likewise.

The net result of this controlled trade and finance, based largely on political and military association, is a considerable commercial as well as strictly war debt owed by Franco Spain to Germany and Italy. Several official business men and bankers have told this writer the commercial debt to those two countries was just over $100,000,000. Of this total, it is said, $75,000,000 is owing to Germany and $30,000,000 to Italy.

Some believe this partly covers war material, but the line between commercial and war debt accounts is difficult to draw, and it is not certain whether even officials have kept the two entirely separate. One German estimate has put the war debt to Germany at $200,000,000. Others have put it higher. Part, perhaps, has been paid by exports. Anyhow it is by shipments of raw materials in future years that the debt is expected by Germans to be amortized.

No official would even indicate the proportions of this debt and so secret have the transactions been kept that few Spaniards have any notion of how great it is. Some even believe munitions have been paid for and the only unpaid debt is the commercial one.

Puts Debt at $100,000,000

"We shall owe Germany and Italy together not much over 1,000,000,000 pesetas [about $100,000,000 at the peseta's external value]," said one of the leading business men who have advised the Franco government from the beginning. "And that is not a great sum after two years of war.

"This figure includes war materials. We have bought destroyers and submarines from Italy, paying 50 per cent in cash in dollars. We have bought 1,200 Fiat trucks from Italy, 1,800 from Ger-

many and 12,000 Fords and Studebakers from the United States.
"We have bought mostly from the United States because the Germans asked too high prices. They have made big profits from wartime trade with us."

Oil and gasoline have all been paid for in cash, according to officials of the monopoly company, called Campsa, probably because the countries supplying oil would not take the risk of granting credits.

Officials say three-fourths of the war supply of oil has come from the United States and the rest has been bought at British and Belgian ports from middlemen.

One of the highest officials in Franco Spain, speaking privately, said all war materials had been paid for already. Questioned further, he changed his statement, saying it was true "generally speaking."

At the Bank of Spain this writer saw a balance sheet indicating that note circulation in April was 3,745,000,000 pesetas in Franco Spain, as compared with 5,483,000,000 pesetas in all Spain when the war began. A private banker, however, thought the present circulation was nearer 5,000,000,000.

A high banking official informed this writer that the total of bank deposits in Franco Spain is now 2,436,000,000 pesetas, whereas in the whole of Spain at the start of the war the total was 1,100,000,000 pesetas. This expansion is explained by pointing out that the stocks of factories and shops are low and imports of nonessentials prohibited; hence merchants and manufacturers cannot invest in stocks but must leave their money in the banks.

Prices appear to have risen 25 to 30 per cent, perhaps more, for the worker who buys in small quantities. But wages have not risen. Hoarding, formerly universal in Spain, is rare now because of doubt about the currency.

Vignettes of Franco Spain

by Harold Callender

GIBRALTAR.

IN CROSSING Franco-controlled Spain from the Bay of Biscay to the Mediterranean one finds odd contrasts. In the north and southeast the marks of shell, bomb and fire are plainly visible in many places; yet in some towns (Salamanca and Seville, for example) one might almost imagine the country was at peace. Everywhere there is an appearance of complete unity; but beneath the surface are many differences which are certain to emerge at the end of the war, and which it is even now difficult to conceal. For Spain has never been really unified and is not likely soon to be.

Neither in the scarred nor in the unscarred areas is there much evidence of physical privation or of financial strain. Many shops—notably those selling textiles and imported goods—are short, indeed almost bereft, of stocks (for Franco Spain is an agricultural country fighting against the chief industrial centers). But food and wine are in general abundant (though Spanish cuisine seems odd without rice); a considerable amount of building, even of houses, has been done; and the flimsy little paper notes which

From the *New York Times Magazine,* June 12, 1938, copyright © 1938, 1966 by The New York Times Company.

have replaced silver still retain some two-thirds of their purchasing power.

The country is remarkably well organized and orderly, subdued if not unified. It is safe to travel anywhere, which has not always been the case. The large number of political prisoners (much too large to please some Franco supporters), and stories of still grimmer punishments, testify to the price paid for this admirable order. The need to keep order with a strong hand is the raison d'être of the Franco movement, which justifies itself by pointing to the disorders of the republican period.

This problem—like those of food supply, finance and organization—has been solved provisionally, on a war basis, for Franco's part of Spain. But if General Franco's forces occupy Barcelona and Madrid, as they have occupied Bilbao and Santander, all these problems will arise again and on a much larger scale. Perhaps Franco's greatest tasks lie ahead; and, as the North discovered when it had defeated the Confederacy, it may prove difficult to solve them by the use of military power alone.

San Sebastian, now the diplomatic capital of Nationalist Spain, has recovered something of its former cosmopolitan atmosphere and become an active and almost gay resort. The hotels around the semicircular bay are filled with guests who travel in large motor cars and demand and receive first-rate food and wines. The Chicote Bar, a refugee from Madrid (like so many others), has no empty chairs, hardly even standing room, at the cocktail hour of 9. P. M. There officers, fresh from the front, talk of the war in complete disregard of the posters which urge discretion for fear of spies. There foreign diplomats and business men exchange ideas. There well-to-do Spaniards while away the time until they may resume possession of textile factories in Barcelona or apartments in Madrid. ("They think we're fighting for them and their property, but they're wrong," said a soldier.)

But the bulk of the 20,000 refugees in San Sebastian live meagerly, sharing houses or apartments of friends, sustained by loans from banks or relatives. They are mostly innocent victims of revolution and war and they believe the Franco regime offers the only hope of re-establishing normal life.

Not far from the big hotels is a military hospital, occupying a former casino. From it emerge convalescent soldiers, some walking with crutches, some with their arms held at awkward angles by plaster of paris, some with bandaged eyes. They seem rather cheerful, finding this seaside town a pleasant place.

In the villages of Elbar, Durango, Amorebieta and what is left of Guernica, west of San Sebastian, there are no big hotels or American bars; only tiny cafes with modest prices. There are hardly any soldiers. But shattered buildings between green hills supply a hint of what modern war may mean for the civilian. The piles of stone which buried many people have been stacked up on the sites where once stood houses and factories. Here peasants, workmen and shopkeepers were bombarded from the air for reasons which remain somewhat obscure to them.

In Guernica the little square lined with trees remains intact, as do the church, a school, a few houses and the ancient oak under which the Basque Diet sat. But there is nothing else left of this town where 6,000 people dwelt and worked. The railway station consists of four walls with nothing inside. The "front-on," where the Basque game of pelota was played, stands gutted. Twisted iron, jagged timbers, remnants of furniture remain as relics of a once tranquil village which symbolized the political tradition of the Basques. People who were there at the time say the town was bombarded from the air for three and one-half hours. An elderly woman who pointed out the oak tree said she had owned a shop and a building, but that they were wrecked and she now lived on the charity of friends. "Served her right," commented one visitor. "The Basques should not have supported the republic." Guernica paid the price of a political error.

Further on, near the village of Larrabezua, stands a white headstone on which is carved: "Hier fiel am 1.6.1937, in Kampf fuer ein nationales Spanien, August Wilmcen, geboren 14.3.1913 zu Krefeld." Wilmcen apparently was a German aviator. He may have been one of those who punished Guernica for its political mistake; anyhow, he must have helped attack Bilbao.

He probably was a quiet young man, like the German youths in uniform whom one meets all over Franco's Spain. Yet these attractive, civilized-looking youngsters born beyond the Rhine dropped explosives upon defenseless Basque civilians in their own ancient land, annihilating Guernica and destroying Basque autonomy in the interest of "National Spain." Much recent European history is implicit in that simple epitaph. Reading it, one feels sorry for Wilmcen, for the Guernica which lies smashed to bits—and for the Europe which still, somewhat precariously, remains intact.

Thanks largely to these same youths, Bilbao has long been in General Franco's hands. They did little damage to the city itself, though a few empty skeletons of villas show where their bombs fell. But the casino on the hill, a once popular pleasure resort, is a mass of ruins. Around Bilbao, extending for many miles over hills and across valleys, is an elaborate string of trenches and fortifications built by the defenders of the city. Some are neatly constructed with timber supports and drainage ditches; some are sheltered by earth and wood against aerial attack; some form concrete blockhouses, roofed over and provided with slits for machinegunners. But Bilbao had no aircraft and no anti-aircraft defenses. So it fell to Franco, supplying him with iron mines, steel works and the principal port on the northern coast of Spain.

The former Jesuit College has now become a military prison, and lately some 4,000 captives were crowded into the completely unfurnished building, where they slept on floors in the clothing they had been captured in several weeks previously. They said they were fairly well fed, and those not wounded appeared healthy enough, although shaves and baths were considered unnecessary luxuries, and the prisoners were consequently a rough-looking crowd.

Motoring over the mountains southward into Castile, one passes a crowd of school children who quickly give the fascist salute. The peasants do the same all through Central Spain. "Only a few months ago they were all doing this," remarked a Spanish observer, clenching his fist in the Communist greeting. "Funny, isn't it?" It hardly seemed likely that the entire population had suddenly been converted to fascism. Motors being scarce in Spain, they probably assumed that anyone in a private car must be of some consequence; so they behaved accordingly.

Beyond this northern coast range one enters an arid plateau dotted with mountain chains, which suggests Arizona. Crossing the plateau, one understands Spaniards who say that what Spain needs most is water.

Burgos, Franco's Castilian capital, sustains the impression of Arizona, in spite of its ancient cathedral, town gate and Casa del Cordon. For dry winds sweep over it, half-finished hotels give it a raw and Wild Western aspect, while ox carts and donkey carts reveal it as really a rural market town, for all its motor cars and uniforms. The principal hotel, the Condestable, is an international center where ambassadors, consuls, military attachés, business men and correspondents of half a dozen countries assemble for lunch or for after-dinner drinks at 11 P.M. Meanwhile the broad Paseo looks like an army on the move, so numerous are the soldiers who walk up and down endlessly, especially just before 10 o'clock dinner. The cafes are overcrowded; the streets of this once quiet provincial town are packed with people; for into Burgos have been suddenly crammed a horde of officials, some carrying on the war, others busily manufacturing red tape.

In room No. 32 at the Hotel Norte y Londres was a notice in German, signed by Captain Spindler, countersigned by Inspector Boemisch, informing German troops of the Condor Legion (in the precise German way) just how much they must tip when occupying that room, which had been set aside for them. Here was another sign of the curious internationalism of Nationalist Spain's war.

In Valladolid, a pleasant modern town on the Castile plain, one was told of a red terror which lasted more than a year; of persecutions, of priests insulted in the streets, of efforts to burn churches. When Franco's troops arrived, many revolutionaries were shot, others imprisoned, others enrolled in the Franco Falange movement (much to the distress of conservatives). "We cannot shoot them all," it was explained.

Here are the headquarters of the Social Auxiliary of the Falange, a remarkable organization directed by Señora Mercedes Sanz which feeds the hungry, cares for needy mothers and children (red or white) and illustrates the sharpened social conscience which the war has brought.

Salamanca, with its classic square, its softish brown cathedral and churches and monasteries which look almost golden in the sunlight, with its ancient university which once was one of the outstanding seats of learning of the world, seems a long way from the war (though it was bombed in January). The atmosphere is pleasantly medieval, inviting repose and contemplation of the richly carved facades and quiet cloisters. But the square is filled with soldiers, the press with the scant war news officially authorized, and everybody's mind is on the progress of Franco's troops.

At the railway station there are no books on sale—Franco's Spain is short of books, for the publishing houses were mostly in Barcelona—but there are newspapers, cigarettes, large loaves of bread, coffee and wine.

In the train soldiers fill the compartments and aisles, sit or lie on the platforms, overflow into the vestibules, so that it is difficult to get in or out. Again nobody seems to mind; everybody is patient and polite; time is no object (the train averages less than twenty miles an hour).

Eventually it reaches Andalusia, with its sedate and tranquil capital, Seville. The arid regions are far behind, and one enters a warm and luxuriant province of olives and oranges and cattle, where peasants live in odd huts made of thatch with one door which suggests the Africa which is so close, both geographically and racially. At Seville and at Jerez are large flying grounds, and war planes may be seen circling in the air. There is a shortage of matches and cloth, and business men grumble at Burgos' bureaucratic meddling. But one eats and drinks well and can come as near forgetting the war as anywhere in Spain.

Yet all think of it; and he who imagines that their views are identical, as the new totalitarian state demands, will find in due course that he is greatly mistaken.

Franco's Spain
Twenty Years Later

by Hugh Trevor-Roper

IT IS NOW twenty years since General Franco launched his "crusade" which ended three years later in the destruction of the Spanish Republic. Since then he has ruled unchallenged as *Caudillo,* or leader, of his country. His survival for so long a period is a remarkable achievement. In spite of a terrible civil war, which has made the origins of his rule seem outrageous to many of his subjects (after all, unlike him, even Hitler and Mussolini obtained power legally), in spite of the overthrow of his foreign protectors, in spite of a long boycott by the Western powers, General Franco remains apparently firm upon his throne.

It is true there have recently been symptoms of unrest; and since in a dictatorship all symptoms are exaggerated in interpretation, some observers have supposed that his regime is in danger. But I do not think this is so. The Government of General Franco may not be popular. It has no institutions to lend it natural permanence. But it has an internal strength (and he himself has a political genius) which, I think, will enable it to survive these lesser crises just as it has survived far greater crises in the past.

What is the nature of this internal strength? Partly it is a nega-

From the *New York Times Magazine,* September 2, 1956, copyright © 1956 by The New York Times Company.

tive strength: the resignation, the exhaustion of his people. To all those who remember it, the civil war of 1936–39 is a dreadful memory. On both sides atrocities were committed which are now recalled with horror, and even those who hate General Franco most for his share in the responsibility accept him now as a guarantee against a renewal of such atrocities.

But this is not the whole explanation. It is equally important to remember that Franco's revolution was not a new "Fascist" revolution. It was a reversion to ancient traditions far more deeply rooted in the country, traditions which, re-established by him, now help to keep him in power although fascism has collapsed.

One only has to look across the frontier to Portugal to see a very similar situation. There, too, a "traditional" dictatorship has been established, and has lasted thirty years. The methods by which Dr. Salazar came to power in Portugal are very different from those which brought Franco to power in Spain. But it is the fact of the restoration of tradition, not the methods, which is ultimately significant.

I have said that Franco's Government is not "Fascist." Of course, it has often been thought to be Fascist, and it was certainly put in power by Hitler and Mussolini. And indeed, as long as he was fighting for power, or thought that he could profit by supporting Hitler and Mussolini, Franco used the language of fascism and gave prominence to the Falange, which had some of the genuine characteristics of a Fascist party. But there can be no doubt that this was mere opportunism. As soon as he could, Franco disembarrassed himself of Fascist protection, reduced the Falange to a mutual benefit society in which the "Fascist" elements were, as they are now, a dissident minority. And he revealed himself to be, not of course a liberal or a democrat—he hates liberalism and democracy—but a regent for an old-style clerical monarchy. This was recognized by Hitler, whom he let down, long before it was recognized by the Allies, who continued to boycott him as a "Fascist" after 1945. Even Communists, Hitler would say in 1942, were more sympathetic to him than "clerical-monarchist muck" like the Government of General Franco, that "inflated peacock" smugly seated on his "pretender's throne."

If Franco is not and in truth never has been a Fascist, it is equally true to say that he never saved Spain from communism, as he himself claims. In fact, in 1936, when he launched his "crusade," there were only two Communist Deputies in the Spanish Parliament, and so little did anyone believe in a Communist menace that Franco himself, in his manifestoes at that time, forgot to mention any such menace.

What he sought to save Spain from was not communism but liberal democracy. It is true that in the course of the struggle the Spanish Communists gradually rose to power on the Republican side, just as the "Fascist" Falange rose to power on Franco's side. But that was a consequence, not a cause, of the struggle. It arose from the fact that Russia was the only power which would supply arms to the Republican Government, and that these arms were supplied through the Communist party. The Republican Government, had it been victorious, might have emancipated itself from such temporary Communist allies as skillfully as General Franco emancipated himself from his temporary Fascist allies. However, since it has become fashionable and profitable to show anti-Communist virtue, Franco would hardly deserve his reputation for statesmanship if he had not now jumped on this universal bandwagon and claimed to have "saved" Spain from communism.

Thus the Government of Spain does not really fit into any familiar twentieth century pattern. It may be described as "Fascist" or "anti-Communist" but in fact it is neither. It is an ancient Bourbon monarchy, with no parallel in the world, and Franco is not really a dictator in the modern sense: he is a regent.

Spain, he declared in his Law of Succession, promulgated in 1947, "is a Catholic, social, representative state which, in accordance with its tradition, is hereby declared to be constitutionally a monarchy." The *Caudillo,* he goes on to say, may "at any moment" nominate his own successor "as King or as Regent." In the meantime, lest they should seem to have fallen into disuse, he himself exercises all the prerogatives of monarchy.

How is it possible that such an archaic system of government has succeeded in reimposing itself in twentieth century Europe? The answer is that Spain, as Napoleon observed, is not Europe.

Spain is part of Africa accidentally attached to Europe. For centuries it was under African domination, and even today it often seems less different from Morocco across the Straits than from France over the Pyrenees. Even after the Moors had been expelled, Spain did not develop along the same lines as Europe. It did not share Europe's intellectual experiences or its economic growth. Consequently it lacks a well-developed middle class and has hardly known either the liberalism of such a class when it is rising or the fascism which is often a symptom of its decline.

Equally, it lacks an organized industrial working class, and has hardly known the socialism or communism of such a class. At least it has not known them as native movements. It has known them only as imported movements against which, sooner or later, the ancient, native conservatism of a rural, clerical, almost static society has been roused to revolt. It revolted in 1809, when the Spanish landlords, peasants and priests rose up and threw out the half absorbed European "Enlightenment"; it revolted again in this century against the half absorbed European democratic liberalism.

To this generalization there is always an important exception, but it is the exception that proves the rule. Catalonia and the Basque country, in the north of Spain, have always been "European" rather than Spanish. When Spain was part of Africa, they were part of France; and today they still remain a "little Europe in Spain," with all the characteristics of European society—a higher standard of life, a liberal middle class, an organized industrial working class. All through Spanish history Catalonia has been the adversary, and has ended by being the victim, of Castile. It is no accident that the Republic made its last stand against Franco in Catalonia, that Franco has since sought to stamp out the language and traditions of Catalonia, or that it is in Catalonia and the Basque country that industrial opposition has recently shown itself. But precisely because of this fact, Franco's victory was no less a victory over Europe for being a victory also over Catalonia.

Such then are the basis and character of Franco's Government, which give it its internal strength. But I have spoken also of Franco's own political genius which also has contributed to its survival. It is not a broad or humane genius; he has been quite unnecessarily vindictive to his defeated opponents. It has nothing intellectual in it. It is rather a sustained political shrewdness elevated by a singular lack of egotism. For Franco has shown himself to have far greater political understanding than anyone expected of him when he first fought his way to power. Inconspicuous, cautious, thinking carefully before acting, but acting promptly after thought, he is generally two moves ahead of his rivals.

He has prevented any rival from approaching his throne. The *Cortes* or Parliament is completely packed and managed by him. Though it can legally reject a Government measure, it has never done so. The Falange is ultimately under his control. He is Generalissimo of the Army. And in these positions he has known how to prevent the emergence of any threat to his own supremacy. He manipulates, balances, cajoles, pensions, in such a way that he alone rules and no one in Spain can now see any alternative to him.

Does this mean that there is no independent life, no opposition, no variety or vitality in modern Spain? That would be a very unfair assumption. There is vitality enough, but it is not now represented in the avowed opposition parties—the *émigré* Liberals, the suppressed Communists. Since political parties are forbidden in Spain, it cannot be expressed in parties at all. It is expressed in "movements," in "tendencies" which seek not to overthrow the regime—that would open the door to civil war—but to transform it from within. Within the Falange, which has now shed its "Fascist" character and become a vast system of patronage, a freemasonry of jobgivers and job-seekers, there is a movement of social radicalism which preserves some of the original idealism of the "crusade." Within the Church there is a Christian Democratic movement, led by Dr. Angel Herrera, Bishop of Málaga, which protests against the materialism and the privileges, some would even say the paganism, of the established Church.

And of course there are many who resent the lack of liberty, the corruption and the illiberalism of a personal regime which, they think, is beneath the dignity of a proud and civilized people. But none of these "movements" wants to displace Franco: they all reckon on achieving their aims by influence, not revolution. They would be happy if he would last, at least until they have completed their plans for the future government of Spain.

But Franco cannot last forever, and it is precisely this fact which lies at the root of all the recent disturbances—the student riots, the murmuring in the Army, the industrial discontent. For Franco, too, has his plans for the future, and he is determined to settle the succession before he retires from the scene. This determination would seem to be to his credit. In fact it is a source of weakness to him.

For if all the restless "movements" in Spain are reconciled to his present rule, that is because its very looseness, its personal, indeterminate character, its lack of institutions leave the future still open. A firm settlement of the succession would close it. Further, Franco wishes to close it by a very controversial act: the restoration, as an institution, of the real Bourbon monarchy. In fact, he has already gone halfway toward such a restoration. In January, 1955, he saw the claimant to the throne, the Count of Barcelona, and reached an agreement with him whereby his son, Don Juan Carlos, should be educated by the Spanish state for the ultimate office of kingship.

Why is the restoration of the Bourbons so controversial in Spain? Why do people who do not resent the exercise of monarchical powers by General Franco apprehend the succession of a more legitimate monarch? The answer lies in the past record of the monarchy, and in the vested interests of the "crusade."

First, there is the opposition of the Falange. The original idealists of the Falange were inspired (as even Fascist idealists were originally inspired) by a certain social radicalism. They hated the "Left"—liberalism, democracy, anarchism—but they also attacked the abuses, the social conservatism, the clericalism, of the old "Right." Now they already feel that Franco, in becoming a clerical monarchist, has half betrayed their ideals; but at least he is obliged by his own past to pay lip service to them. A real king, they think, would jettison the Falange altogether, and that would mean not only a blow against social reform but also financial loss for all those hangers-on who constitute 90 per cent of that great system of jobbery into which the disillusioned Falange has now degenerated.

Other supporters of Franco fear that the monarchy may prove to be a "constitutional" monarchy like the British monarchy, which will allow the return of that liberal democracy which Franco himself overthrew. And the Christian Democrats fear that the monarchy will mean government by the monarchist classes—the traditional upper classes whose privileged irresponsibility is one of their regular themes.

Thus it can be said that Franco's own supporters are seriously disconcerted by the program of restoration, and those who favor such a program are largely the enemies of Franco—the liberals and republicans who see in the monarchy, at best, a means toward "constitutionalism" or, at worst, a weaker adversary than the *Caudillo*.

Of course Franco has done his best to reassure his supporters. In repeated statements, in which he has recognized the "dismay" which the project has caused among "our friends," he has explained that the monarchy will not be "constitutional" but "social and popular." These assurances, however, have not been sufficient to calm the general apprehension.

In June last year the Secretary General of the Falange publicly declared that his "movement" could not support the monarchy unless the monarchy first guaranteed the continued existence of the Falange. In March of this year came the students' riots, as a result of which Franco dismissed the Secretary General of the Falange, the Minister of Education, and the rector of the university (himself a Falangist idealist).

Soon afterward Franco had to face other difficulties. First he decided to give up the Spanish Protectorate in Morocco. This, I believe, was a wise decision; but it has caused dismay among many officers in the Army, which is, after all, the mainstay of the regime. Secondly, he found himself faced by industrial opposition in the north, where the workers in many factories went on strike, although strikes are illegal in Spain. By mid-April it seemed that Franco was in serious difficulty.

However, I do not think that General Franco has lost his nerve.

Already he has shown what his new course is to be. He is turning seriously to the social problem. Labor questions have been subordinated to the Falange, and the new Secretary General of the Falange, in his first public speech, outlined future policy as "winning over the workers and settling the future form of government."

In other words, Franco has not given up his plan to restore the monarchy. But he has seen the red light. He is trying, by a reconciliation with the Falange, to sell the monarchy to it and then, through it, by new social legislation, to the workers. In this way he hopes to live up to his promise, or at least to give plausibility to his promise, that the restored Bourbon monarchy will be not irresponsible and reactionary but "social and popular."

Will he succeed? It is impossible to say. Much will depend on time and accident. Even if General Franco preserves his own power to the end, it may well be that the Spaniards will prefer either a Presidential Republic to continue his form of government or a "constitutional" monarchy to replace it. But there can be no doubt what General Franco himself wants.

Long ago, as an officer, he swore an oath of loyalty to Alfonso XIII, whose memory he has always defended. He has now enjoyed a long personal reign as regent. If he can close his own reign by placing upon the throne a real Spanish prince brought up in the old pre-constitutional tradition, then he will die happy with a *Nunc Dimittis*.

Suggested Reading

Franz Borkenau, *The Spanish Cockpit,* Ann Arbor, University of Michigan Press, 1963 (paperback).

Gerald Brenan, *The Spanish Labyrinth,* New York, Cambridge University Press, 1943 (paperback).

David T. Cattell, *Communism and the Spanish Civil War,* New York, Russell and Russell, 1965.

Robert G. Colodny, *The Struggle for Madrid,* New York, Paine-Whitman, 1958.

Lawrence Fernsworth, *Spain's Struggle for Freedom,* Boston, Beacon Press, 1957.

Allen Guttman, *The Wound in the Heart,* New York, Free Press, 1962.

Ernest Hemingway, *For Whom the Bell Tolls,* New York, Scribner's, 1943 (paperback).

Gabriel Jackson, *The Spanish Republic and the Civil War,* Princeton, Princeton University Press, 1965 (paperback).

André Malraux, *Man's Hope,* New York, Random House, 1938 (Bantam paperback).

Herbert L. Matthews, *Two Wars and More to Come,* New York, Carrick and Evans, 1938.

George Orwell, *Homage to Catalonia,* New York, Harcourt Brace, 1952 (paperback).

Stanley G. Payne, *Falange: A History of Spanish Fascism,* Stanford, Stanford University Press, 1961 (paperback).

Stanley G. Payne, *The Spanish Revolution,* New York, W. W. Norton, 1970 (paperback).

√ Dante Puzzo, *Spain and the Great Powers, 1936–1941,* New York, Columbia University Press, 1962.

Gustav Regler, *The Great Crusade,* New York, Longmans Green, 1940.

J. W. D. Trythall, *Franco,* London, Rupert Hart-Davis, 1970.

Index

Alberche River, 102
Alcazar, 8–9, 104
Alfonso XIII, 4, 25, 32, 36–37, 138, 170, 184, 203
Alicante, 79
Almeria, 32, 78–79; bombing of, 153–154, 159, 165–166, 168, 170–172, 175
Alvarez, Melquiades, 122
Alvarez del Vayo, Julio, 112–114, 162–163
America, 64, 67; investments in Spain, 156; and trade with Spain, 14, 183, 189
American Friends Service Committee (Quakers), 75, 78–79
Anarchism, 90, 133, 138; definition of, 134–137; goals of, 137
Anarchists, 48, 134, 139, 141–142; and the defense of Madrid, 9, 108; and the Republic, 4–6, 15–17, 90, 129–132, 142, 150
Anarcho-syndicalism, 27, 91; definition of, 138; and the Republic, 112, 114
Anarcho-Syndicalist Workers Confederation, 150
Andalusia, 4, 6–7, 72, 139, 195
Aragon, 6, 71, 176; and anarchism, 135; battle of, 17; and collectivization, 11, 16, 91

Aranjuez, 62
Aravaca, 66
Asensio, José, 113–114
Asturias, 61; revolt in, 3 5, 41, 97, 127
Austria, 104, 116
Azaña, Manuel, 5, 29, 37, 71, 112, 127, 143; and Franco, 24; resignation of, 19, 91, 151

Badajoz, 8, 46
Bakunin, Mikhail, 91, 136
Balearic Islands, 25, 171
Barcelona, 13, 16, 25, 44, 121, 125–126, 128, 131, 136, 138, 140, 157, 191, 195; occupation of, 19, 81–87; uprising in, 6, 90; wartime conditions in, 77
Barroso, Antonio, 65–66
Basques, 6, 11, 13–15, 28, 90, 131, 192–193, 199
Beimler, Hans, 97
Belchite, 176
Belgium: investments in Spain, 155–157; trade with Spain, 183, 189
Bellver, 139
Besteiro, Julián, 19, 169; and National Defense Council, 150–151
Bilbao, 6, 32, 61, 73, 156, 191, 193; battle of, 13–15, 164

Biscay, Bay of, 176
Blum, Léon, 7, 10, 26, 32
Boadilla, 66
Brihuega, 63, 73
Brunete, Battle of, 14, 20, 43, 63–70
Buck, Tim, 93–94
Bujaraloz, 135
Burgos, 32, 72, 194–195

Cacares, 32, 70
Calvo Sotelo, José, 21, 25, 27; assassination of, 6
Cambo, Francisco, 142
Canary Islands, 6, 25, 27
Carabanchel, 66
Carlists, 4, 12, 14, 28, 126
Carrillo, Wenceslao, 150
Cartagena, 149–150, 156
Casado, Segismundo: and Council of National Defense, 19, 91, 149–150, 152
Caspe, 144
Castile, 4, 6, 28, 104, 193, 199
Castillo, José, 6
Catalonia, 25, 28, 32, 78, 84, 127, 130–131, 140, 142; and anarchism, 135, 139; autonomy movement in, 3–4, 6, 16, 18; and collectivization, 11, 16, 91, 141; history of, 199; occupation of, 18–19, 151; and the POUM, 16; revolt in, 5, 132
Catholic Church, 4, 14–15, 17–18, 38–39, 198–200
Ceuta, 24
Chamberlain, Neville, 176
Chatfield, Alfred Ernle Monacute, 176
Civil Guards, 11, 28, 48, 87
Claridad, 107, 124
CNT. *See* National Confederation of Labor.
Collectivist revolution, 11, 16
Communism, 25, 28, 133–134; definition of, 135–136
Communist International. *See* Third International.

Communists, 4, 16–17, 19, 90, 133, 139; and Franco's regime, 198, 200; with the International Brigades, 93–95, 99–100, 104; and the Negrín government, 129–131; and the Popular Front, 5, 142, 184; and the POUM, 126–128; and the defense of Madrid, 9, 108. *See also* Popular Front.
Companys, Luis, 91, 126, 140
Confederation of Autonomous Right parties, 4
Congress of Saragossa, 136
Cordova, 32
Council of National Defense. *See* National Defense Council.
Cuenca, 32
Czechoslovakia, 96

Delbos, Yvon, 179, 181
Deutsch, Julius, 116
Deutschland, the, 153, 160–163, 165, 168, 171, 175
Durango, 13, 192

Ebro River offensive, 7–19, 20, 151
Eden, Anthony, 176
Elbar, 192
El Escorial, 63, 65–66
El Ferrol, 156
El Pardo, 65
El Plantio, 66
England. *See* Great Britain.
Escuder Poverell, José, 126

FAI. *See* Iberian Anarchist Federation.
Falange, 4, 11–12, 14, 18, 147, 194, 197–198, 200–203
Fanelli, Giuseppi, 91
Fascism, 21, 23, 25–27, 29, 39–40, 42, 89, 92, 130–131, 134–135; and Franco's regime, 197–198; International Brigades and, 95, 100; Russia and, 8, 166–168
Fatarella, 139
Ferrer, Francisco, 91, 138

Foreign Legion, 8, 24, 33, 41, 43, 46, 48–49, 104
France, 14, 34, 153–154; and aid to the Republic, 7, 31–33, 104, 111; and the bombing of Almeria, 168; and the *Deutschland* incident, 159–160; and the International Brigades, 96, 104, 115; and investments in Spain, 155–157; and the Nyon Conference, 175–181
Franco, Francisco, 5, 9, 18–19, 24–25, 29, 33, 46, 92, 113, 140, 148; and Axis support, 7, 145–146, 162; and the Battle of Brunete, 64–65, 68, 70; and the battle for Teruel, 17, 71; and the Bilbao offensive, 164; and the *Deutschland* incident, 153–154; early victories of, 72–73; and the International Brigades, 94, 100; military advantages of, 74; military strategy of, 8, 34, 49–51, 89–90; and the occupation of Barcelona, 81, 84–86; regime of, 14–15, 18, 183–184, 191, 196–200; and the restoration of the monarchy, 201–203; and the siege of Madrid, 103–106, 113–114. *See also* Nationalists.

Galan, Francisco, 149
Galicia, 6
Galliani, Umberto, 96
General Union of Workers (UGT), 4–5, 7, 9, 11–12, 26, 130, 139, 150
Germany, 32, 92, 145–147, 158; and aid to Nationalists, 7, 9–11, 13, 18, 21, 49, 73–74, 104, 162; and the bombing of Almeria, 153–154, 159, 165, 168, 170; and the *Deutschland* incident, 153, 160–161, 163, 165, 168, 171–172; and the International Brigades, 96, 104, 111; and investments in Spain, 155–157; and

the Nyon Conference, 174–175; and trade with Spain, 14, 183, 186–189
Gibraltar, 7, 72
Gijon, 14, 73, 176
Gil Robles, José María, 5–6, 22, 27, 40, 142
Giral, José, 7, 30–31, 112
Goded, Manuel, 25, 29
Granada, 50, 135, 148
Great Britain, 7, 10, 15, 32, 153–154; and the *Deutschland* incident, 159–160, 168, 171; and the International Brigades, 104, 111; and investments in Spain, 155–157; and the Nyon Conference, 173–181; and trade with Spain, 14, 183
Guadalajara, 13, 32, 73, 147
Guadarrama River, 63
Guernica, 13, 192–193
Gwinner, Arthur von, 157

Heinemann, Dannie, 157
Heinemann, Elkan, 157
Herrera, Angel, 200
Hitler, Adolf, 7–8, 17–18, 145–146, 163–165, 175, 196–197
Hospitalet, 84, 86

Iberian Anarchist Federation (FAI), 130, 138–139
Insurgents. *See* Nationalists.
International Alliance of Socialist Democracy, 136
International Brigades, 10, 66, 72–73, 89–90, 93–100, 104, 111, 116
Irun, 73
Italy, 32, 92, 145–147, 153–154, 158–159; and aid to Nationalists, 7, 9–11, 13, 15, 21, 49, 73, 104, 162; and the *Deutschland* incident, 163, 165, 168, 172; and the International Brigades, 95, 104, 111; and investments in Spain, 155–156; and the Nyon Conference, 173–177, 180; and trade with Spain, 183, 186, 188

Jarama River, 13, 20
Jerez, 195
Johnson, John D., 119
Juan Carlos, 184, 201
Juan de Bourbon (the Pretender), 184

Kerensky, Alexander, 29, 41
Kleber, Emilio, 93–96, 116
Kupinsky, Wolf, 126

La Batalla, 126
La Carraca, 156
Largo Caballero, Francisco, 26, 107, 124, 170; and the Anarchists, 129–130; government of, 15–16, 90, 103, 112–113, 169; and the Negrín government, 131–132
Las Rozas, 66
Law of Succession. *See* Succession, Law of.
Lerroux, Alejandro, 23, 122
Lliga Catalana, 142
Llobregat River, 82
Lluna Pujols, José, 137
Lorenzo, Anselmo, 137
Loyalists. *See* Republic.

MacKenzie, David, 98–99
Madariaga, Salvador de, 134
Madrid, 6, 25, 32–34, 49–51, 78, 125–126, 128, 131–132, 136, 149, 151, 191; and the Battle of Brunete, 63–65, 69–70; siege of, 10, 12–14, 19–20, 43, 52–62, 72–73, 89–90, 92, 94, 101–124, 169–170
Majadahonda, 67
Majorca, 6
Malaga, 13, 50, 73, 78, 169
Malatesta, Errico, 137–138
Malraux, André, 99
Manzanares River, 105–106
Marin, Gonzales, 150
Martinez de Valasco, José, 122
Martinez Varrio, Diego, 169
Marty, André, 100
Matagorda, 156

Matallana, Manuel, 19
Mateu, Miguel, 87
Maurín, Joaquín, 90, 127
Mella, Ricardo, 137
Men of the Republic, 37–39, 41
Miaja, José, 10, 19, 62, 69, 116, 142, 150, 169
Mola, Emilio, 9, 33–34, 49–50, 168
Monarchists, 4, 6, 18, 25, 30, 157, 202
Moors, 8, 24, 41, 47–49, 67, 69, 104, 148, 199
Morocco, 3, 6–7, 31, 50–51, 72, 81–83, 183, 185, 199, 202
Mostoles, 66
Murcia, 78–79
Mussolini, Benito, 7, 15, 96, 145–146, 154, 159, 161, 163–164, 196–197

National Confederation of Labor (CNT), 5, 7, 11–12, 26, 130–131, 138–139
National Defense Council, 19, 149–151
Nationalist Law of Political Responsibilities, 19
Nationalists (Insurgents), 6, 14, 30, 34, 46–48, 89, 93, 127, 169, 173; and Axis support, 10, 12, 74, 154 (*see also* Germany, Italy); and battle for Bilbao, 13–14, 61; and Battle of Brunete, 63–70; and battle for Teruel, 17, 73–74; and the capture of Aragon, 17; and the capture of Gijon, 14; and the capture of Santander, 14; and the capture of Toledo, 102, 113; and the *Deutschland* incident, 168; early victories of, 8, 72; and the Ebro River offensive, 19; and financing of the war, 186–189; and foreign investors, 153, 155–157; and the Nyon Conference, 176, 180; and the occupation of Barcelona, 44, 81–87; and the occupation of Catalonia, 18–19, 151; and the occu-

pation of Tarragona, 19; and Portugal, 10–11, 13, 21; and the siege of Madrid, 9–10, 12–14, 20, 56–57, 62, 90, 104–108, 111, 169–170; and the uprising at Cartagena, 149–150; zone, conditions in, 11–12, 43–44, 75–77, 190–195. *See also* Alcazar; Almeria, bombing of; *Deutschland;* Franco, Francisco; Nyon Conference.

Navalagamella, 63
Navalcarnero, 62–64, 69–70
Navarre, 6, 28, 81–83
Negrín, Juan, 16–19, 143; government of, 61, 90–91, 129–133, 135, 152, 169; and National Defense Council, 149 151
Nenni, Pietro, 96
Neurath, Constantin von, 163
New Castile, 11
Nin, Andrés, 16–17, 90, 125–128, 131–132
Non-Intervention Committee, 11, 15, 115, 153, 165, 168–169
Nonintervention policy, 10, 20, 155
Nyon Conference, 15, 154, 173, 175–181

Oehler, Hugo, 126
Official Gazette, 85, 151
Orr, Charles, 126
Ortíz, Julio Gomez, 126
Oviedo, 73, 76

Pacciardi, Randolfo, 95–96
Palma, Majorca, 74
Pius XI, Pope, 146
Poland, 96, 104, 111
Popular Front (French), 7–8, 10, 162
Popular Front (Spanish), 5–6, 8, 11, 19, 23, 26–28, 30, 34, 41, 90, 112, 142, 184
Portela Valladares, Manuel, 142
Portugal, 7, 9–11, 13, 21, 197
POUM. *See* United Marxist Workers Party.
Pouritch, Bozidar, 178

Pozuelo, 66, 96
Prieto, Indalecio, 26, 131, 143
Primo de Rivera, Miguel, 3, 18, 24–25, 37–39, 138
Puigcerda, 139

Quakers. *See* American Friends Service Committee.
Queipo de Llano, Gonzalo, 7, 62
Quijorna, 63–65
Quiroga, Santiago, 24

Red Cross, International, 90
Regler, Gustav, 97
Republic (Loyalists), 19, 23–24, 31, 33–34, 43–44, 48, 51, 70, 75, 173; and the Anarchists, 130, 133, 139, and the battle for Aragon, 17; and the Battle of Brunete, 13–14, 43, 63–70; and the bombing of Almeria, 154, 170–172; censorship by, 101, 117–118; and the *Deutschland* incident, 153, 162, 168, 171, 175; and the Ebro River offensive, 17, 19; early battles, 72–73; and foreign investors, 153, 155–157; and French support, 7, 10, 97, 104; government of, 9, 11, 15–16, 21, 29, 74, 89, 91, 120, 142–143, 169; history of, 4–6, 36–42, 134; and the International Brigades, 93, 95, 98, 104; and the loss of Barcelona, 82–85; and the National Defense Council, 149–151; and the Nyon Conference, 176–180; and the siege of Madrid, 13, 61–62, 104–109, 111–114; and the Teruel offensive, 17, 71, 73. *See also* Alcazar; Communists; Negrín, Juan; Nin, Andrés; Popular Front; POUM; Russia, aid to the Republic.
Republic, Men of the. *See* Men of the Republic.
Rojo, Vicente, 10, 19, 62, 142
Romilly, Esmond, 98–99
Rosenberg, Marcel, 112–115
Rovira, José, 128

Russia, 92, 145, 159, 162; aid to the Republic, 9, 11, 15, 18–19, 73, 104, 111–116, 198; and the bombing of Almeria, 166; and the *Deutschland* incident, 153, 160; and fascism, 166–168; and the International Brigades, 90, 104; and investments in Spain, 155; and the Nyon Conference, 174–177, 179. *See also* International Brigades.

Salamanca, 32, 72, 190, 195
Salas, Javier de, 122–123
San Andrés, Miguel, 150
Sanjurjo y Sacanell, José, 3, 25
San Martín de Valdeiglesias, 63
San Sebastian, 32, 73, 191
Santander, 14, 61, 64–65, 191
Serrano y Oteiza, Juan, 137
Sesena, 62–64
Sevilla la Nueva, 66
Seville, 7, 28, 32, 50, 72, 146, 190, 195
Sierra front, 9, 63, 66, 69, 130
Socialism, 42, 133, 135
Socialists, 4, 9, 16–17, 39–40, 48; and the International Brigades, 93, 96; and the National Defense Council, 150; and the Negrín government, 130–131; and the Popular Front, 5–6, 90, 139. *See also* Popular Front.
Solmssen, Georg, 157
Sorel, Georges, 138
Soviet Union. *See* Russia.
Stalin, Joseph, 8, 16
Succession, Law of, 198
Syndicalism. *See* Anarcho-syndicalism.

Tagus River, 64
Talavera, 8, 47
Tarragona, 19
Terrorism, 11–12, 46, 194; Loyalists and, 90, 122–123; Nationalists and, 6–7, 13, 43, .51

Teruel, battle of, 17, 20, 43, 71–74
Third International, 8, 112, 126
Toledo, 121; battle of, 32, 50, 102, 104, 113
Tortosa, 70
Trotsky, Leon, 90, 116, 126, 127–128

UGT. *See* General Union of Workers.
Ultima Hora, 126
Unamuno, Miguel de, 27
United Marxist Workers Party (POUM), 16–17, 90, 125–128, 130–131
United States. *See* America.
Urales, Federico, 135
Usera, 70

Valdemorillo, 63
Valencia, 11, 32, 71, 91, 128, 131, 138–139, 151; government moves to, 103, 112, 114, 116, 120
Valencian government. *See* Republic.
Valladolid, 32, 194
Valls, Eduardo, 150
Vansittart, Sir Robert, 176
Varela, Lopez, 50
Vatican. *See* Catholic Church.
Villafranca del Castillo, 67
Villanueva de la Cañada, 63–66
Villanueva del Pardillo, 61–63, 67
Villaverde, 66, 70
Villaviciosa, 66
Vitoria, 32

Weissgaerber, Alois, 99
Wendelin, Eric, 120

Yague, Juan, 82

Zaharoff, Basil, 156
Zamora, 32

A Note on the Editor

Gabriel Jackson's *The Spanish Republic and the Civil War* won the Adams Prize of the American Historical Assocation as the best book in European history for 1966, and established his reputation as a leading interpreter of this crucial moment in the twentieth century. Mr. Jackson has since written *Historian's Quest* and *The Making of Medieval Spain*. Born in Mount Vernon, New York, he studied at Harvard, Stanford, and the University of Toulouse (France). He is now Professor of History at the University of California, San Diego.

QUADRANGLE PAPERBACKS

American History

James Truslow Adams. *Provincial Society, 1690-1763.* (QP403)
Frederick Lewis Allen. *The Lords of Creation.* (QP35)
Lewis Atherton. *Main Street on the Middle Border.* (QP36)
Thomas A. Bailey. *Woodrow Wilson and the Lost Peace.* (QP1)
Thomas A. Bailey. *Woodrow Wilson and the Great Betrayal.* (QP2)
Charles A. Beard. *The Idea of National Interest.* (QP27)
Carl L. Becker. *Everyman His Own Historian.* (QP33)
Barton J. Bernstein. *Politics and Policies of the Truman Administration.* (QP72)
Ray A. Billington. *The Protestant Crusade.* (QP12)
Allan G. Bogue. *From Prairie to Corn Belt.* (QP50)
Kenneth E. Boulding. *The Organizational Revolution.* (QP43)
Robert V. Bruce. *1877: Year of Violence.* (QP73)
Roger Burlingame. *Henry Ford.* (QP76)
Gerald M. Capers. *John C. Calhoun, Opportunist.* (QP70)
David M. Chalmers. *Hooded Americanism.* (QP51)
John Chamberlain. *Farewell to Reform.* (QP19)
Arthur C. Cole. *The Irrepressible Conflict, 1850-1865.* (QP407)
Alice Hamilton Cromie. *A Tour Guide to the Civil War.*
Robert D. Cross. *The Emergence of Liberal Catholicism in America.* (QP44)
Richard M. Dalfiume. *American Politics Since 1945.* (NYTimes Book, QP57)
Carl N. Degler. *The New Deal.* (NYTimes Book, QP74)
Chester McArthur Destler. *American Radicalism, 1865-1901.* (QP30)
Robert A. Divine. *American Foreign Policy Since 1945.* (NYTimes Book, QP58)
Robert A. Divine. *Causes and Consequences of World War II.* (QP63)
Robert A. Divine. *The Cuban Missile Crisis.* (QP86)
Robert A. Divine. *The Illusion of Neutrality.* (QP45)
Elisha P. Douglass. *Rebels and Democrats.* (QP26)
Melvyn Dubofsky. *American Labor Since the New Deal.* (NYTimes Book, QP87)
Arthur A. Ekirch, Jr. *Ideologies and Utopias.* (QP89)
Harold U. Faulkner. *The Quest for Social Justice, 1898-1914.* (QP411)
Carl Russell Fish. *The Rise of the Common Man, 1830-1850.* (QP406)
Felix Frankfurter. *The Commerce Clause.* (QP16)
Lloyd C. Gardner. *Architects of Illusion.* (QP91)
Edwin Scott Gaustad. *The Great Awakening in New England.* (QP46)
Ray Ginger. *Altgeld's America.* (QP21)
Ray Ginger. *Modern American Cities.* (NYTimes Book, QP67)
Ray Ginger. *Six Days or Forever?* (QP68)
Evarts B. Greene. *The Revolutionary Generation, 1763-1790.* (QP404)
Gerald N. Grob. *Workers and Utopia.* (QP61)
Louis Hartz. *Economic Policy and Democratic Thought.* (QP52)
William B. Hesseltine. *Lincoln's Plan of Reconstruction.* (QP41)
Granville Hicks. *The Great Tradition.* (QP62)
Stanley P. Hirshson. *Farewell to the Bloody Shirt.* (QP53)
Dwight W. Hoover. *A Teacher's Guide to American Urban History.* (QP83)
Dwight W. Hoover. *Understanding Negro History.* (QP49)
Frederic C. Howe. *The Confessions of a Reformer.* (QP39)
Harold L. Ickes. *The Autobiography of a Curmudgeon.* (QP69)
William Loren Katz. *Teachers' Guide to American Negro History.* (QP210)
Burton Ira Kaufman. *Washington's Farewell Address.* (QP64)
Edward Chase Kirkland. *Dream and Thought in the Business Community, 1860-1900.* (QP11)
Edward Chase Kirkland. *Industry Comes of Age.* (QP42)
Herbert S. Klein. *Slavery in the Americas.* (QP84)
Adrienne Koch. *The Philosophy of Thomas Jefferson.* (QP17)
Gabriel Kolko. *The Triumph of Conservatism.* (QP40)
Aileen S. Kraditor. *Up from the Pedestal.* (QP77)
John Allen Krout and Dixon Ryan Fox. *The Completion of Independence, 1790-1830.* (QP405)
Walter LaFeber. *John Quincy Adams and American Continental Empire.* (QP23)
Lawrence H. Leder. *The Meaning of the American Revolution.* (NYTimes Book, QP66)
Jerome Levinson and Juan de Onís. *The Alliance That Lost Its Way.* (QP92)
David E. Lilienthal. *TVA: Democracy on the March.* (QP28)

American History (continued)

Arthur S. Link. *Wilson the Diplomatist.* (QP18)
Arthur S. Link. *Woodrow Wilson: A Brief Biography.* (QP93)
Huey P. Long. *Every Man a King.* (QP8)
Gene M. Lyons. *America: Purpose and Power.* (QP24)
Neill Macaulay. *The Sandino Affair.* (QP82)
Ernest R. May. *The World War and American Isolation, 1914-1917.* (QP29)
Henry F. May. *The End of American Innocence.* (QP9)
Thomas J. McCormick. *China Market.* (QP75)
August Meier and Elliott Rudwick. *Black Protest in the Sixties.* (NYTimes Book, QP78)
George E. Mowry. *The California Progressives.* (QP6)
Allan Nevins. *The Emergence of Modern America, 1865-1878.* (QP408)
William L. O'Neill. *American Society Since 1945.* (NYTimes Book, QP59)
William L. O'Neill. *Everyone Was Brave.* (QP88)
William L. O'Neill. *The Woman Movement.* (QP80)
William L. O'Neill. *Women at Work.* (QP90)
Frank L. Owsley. *Plain Folk of the Old South.* (QP22)
Thomas G. Paterson. *Cold War Critics.* (QP85)
David Graham Phillips. *The Treason of the Senate.* (QP20)
Julius W. Pratt. *Expansionists of 1898.* (QP15)
Herbert I. Priestley. *The Coming of the White Man, 1492-1848.* (QP401)
C. Herman Pritchett. *The Roosevelt Court.* (QP71)
Moses Rischin. *The American Gospel of Success.* (QP54)
John P. Roche. *The Quest for the Dream.* (QP47)
Arthur Meier Schlesinger. *The Rise of the City, 1878-1898.* (QP410)
David A. Shannon. *The Socialist Party of America.* (QP38)
Andrew Sinclair. *The Available Man.* (QP60)
Preston W. Slosson. *The Great Crusade and After, 1914-1928.* (QP412)
June Sochen. *The Black Man and the American Dream.* (QP81)
John Spargo. *The Bitter Cry of the Children.* (QP55)
Bernard Sternsher. *Hitting Home.* (QP79)
Bernard Sternsher. *The Negro in Depression and War.* (QP65)
Ida M. Tarbell. *The Nationalizing of Business, 1878-1898.* (QP409)
Richard W. Van Alstyne. *The Rising American Empire.* (QP25)
Willard M. Wallace. *Appeal to Arms.* (QP10)
Norman Ware. *The Industrial Worker, 1840-1860.* (QP13)
Dixon Wecter. *The Age of the Great Depression, 1929-1941.* (QP413)
Albert K. Weinberg. *Manifest Destiny.* (QP3)
Bernard A. Weisberger. *They Gathered at the River.* (QP37)
Thomas J. Wertenbaker. *The First Americans, 1607-1690.* (QP402)
Robert H. Wiebe. *Businessmen and Reform.* (QP56)
William Appleman Williams. *The Contours of American History.* (QP34)
William Appleman Williams. *The Great Evasion.* (QP48)
Esmond Wright. *Causes and Consequences of the American Revolution.* (QP31)

European History

William Sheridan Allen. *The Nazi Seizure of Power.* (QP302)
Hans W. Gatzke. *European Diplomacy Between Two Wars, 1919-1939.* (QP351)
Nathanael Greene. *European Socialism Since World War I.* (NYTimes Book, QP309)
W. O. Henderson. *The Industrial Revolution in Europe.* (QP303)
Raul Hilberg. *The Destruction of the European Jews.* (QP301)
Raul Hilberg. *Documents of Destruction.* (QP311)
Gabriel Jackson. *The Spanish Civil War.* (NYTimes Book, QP313)
Richard N. Hunt. *German Social Democracy.* (QP306)
John F. Naylor. *Britain, 1919-1970.* (NYTimes Book, QP312)
Steven E. Ozment. *The Reformation in Medieval Perspective.* (QP350)
Percy Ernst Schramm. *Hitler: The Man and the Military Leader.* (QP308)
Telford Taylor. *Sword and Swastika.* (QP304)
John Weiss. *Nazis and Fascists in Europe, 1918-1945.* (NYTimes Book, QP305)

Social Science

E. Digby Baltzell. *Philadelphia Gentlemen*. (QP236)
Milton L. Barron. *The Blending American*. (QP243)
Abraham S. Blumberg. *Criminal Justice*. (QP227)
James V. Cornehls. *Economic Development and Economic Growth*. (NYTimes Book, QP240)
Donald R. Cressey. *Crime and Criminal Justice*. (NYTimes Book, QP233)
Shalom Endleman. *Violence in the Streets*. (QP215)
Nathan Glazer. *Cities in Trouble*. (NYTimes Book, QP212)
William J. Goode. *The Contemporary American Family*. (NYTimes Book, QP223)
George and Eunice Grier. *Equality and Beyond*. (QP204)
F. William Howton. *Functionaries*. (QP232)
Morris Janowitz. *Political Conflict*. (QP226)
Michael B. Kane. *Minorities in Textbooks*. (QP231)
Kurt Lang and Gladys Engel Lang. *Politics and Television*. (QP216)
Charles O. Lerche, Jr. *Last Chance in Europe*. (QP207)
Raymond W. Mack. *Prejudice and Race Relations*. (NYTimes Book, QP217)
Harry T. Marmion. *The Case Against a Volunteer Army*. (QP234)
David Mitrany. *A Working Peace System*. (QP205)
Wilbert E. Moore. *Technology and Social Change*. (NYTimes Book, QP241)
Earl Finbar Murphy. *Governing Nature*. (QP228)
H. L. Nieburg. *In the Name of Science*. (QP218)
Martin Oppenheimer. *The Urban Guerrilla*. (QP219)
Martin Oppenheimer and George Lakey. *A Manual for Direct Action*. (QP202)
James Parkes. *Antisemitism*. (QP213)
Fred Powledge. *To Change a Child*. (QP209)
Lee Rainwater. *And the Poor Get Children*. (QP208)
The Rockefeller Report on the Americas. (QP214)
Edward Sagarin. *Odd Man In*. (QP242)
Ben B. Seligman. *Main Currents in Modern Economics*. (3 vols, QP237, 238, 239)
Ben B. Seligman. *Molders of Modern Thought*. (NYTimes Book, QP224)
Ben B. Seligman. *Permanent Poverty*. (QP229)
Clarence Senior. *The Puerto Ricans*. (QP201)
Harold L. Sheppard. *Poverty and Wealth in America*. (NYTimes Book, QP220)
Arthur L. Stinchcombe. *Rebellion in a High School*. (QP211)
Edward G. Stockwell. *Population and People*. (QP230)
Harry M. Trebing. *The Corporation in the American Economy*. (NYTimes Book, QP221)
Michael Walzer. *Political Action*. (QP235)
David Manning White. *Pop Culture in America*. (NYTimes Book, QP222)
Harold Wolozin. *American Fiscal and Monetary Policy*. (NYTimes Book, QP225)

Philosophy

F. H. Bradley. *The Presuppositions of Critical History*. (QP108)
E. M. Cioran. *The Temptation to Exist*. (QP119)
William Earle. *The Autobiographical Consciousness*. (QP121)
William Earle. *Objectivity*. (QP109)
James M. Edie, James P. Scanlan, Mary-Barbara Zeldin, George L. Kline. *Russian Philosophy*. (3 vols, QP111, 112, 113)
James M. Edie. *An Invitation to Phenomenology*. (QP103)
James M. Edie. *New Essays in Phenomenology*. (QP114)
James M. Edie. *Phenomenology in America*. (QP105)
R. O. Elveton. *The Phenomenology of Husserl*. (QP116)
Manfred S. Frings. *Heidegger and the Quest for Truth*. (QP107)
Moltke S. Gram. *Kant: Disputed Questions*. (QP104)
James F. Harris, Jr., and Richard Severens. *Analyticity*. (QP117)
E. D. Klemke. *Studies in the Philosophy of G. E. Moore*. (QP115)
Lionel Rubinoff. *Faith and Reason*. (QP106)
Stuart F. Spicker. *The Philosophy of the Body*. (QP118)
Pierre Thévenaz. *What Is Phenomenology?* (QP101)
Paul Tibbetts. *Perception*. (QP110)
Robert E. Wood. *The Future of Metaphysics*. (QP120)